# SO, WHO ARE YOU ANYWAY?



A Mother's Journey through Mental Health, Uncertainty and Healing through Writing

By Sarah Rosse

*Edited by Word Wise Writing Services*
*Designed by Rove Creative*

NATIONAL
LIBRARY OF AUSTRALIA

A catalogue record for this book is available from the National Library of Australia.

**This book is dedicated to my sons,**

For your courage, your resilience, and your hearts that continue to teach me more than I could ever teach you. This book is for you—for the times we've navigated together, for the lessons we've learned, and for the love that carries us forward. May you always know that your stories matter, that your voices are heard, and that you are endlessly cherished.

## TRIGGER WARNING

This book does have themes of mental health, isolation and suicide.

If this content raises concerns with you, please reach out to someone who can support you;

**Lifeline**

Call: 13 11 14

Text: 0477 13 11 14

Website: lifeline.org.au

**Suicide Callback Service**

Call: 1300 659 467

Website: suicidecallbackservice.org.au

**Beyond Blue**

Call: 1300 224 636

Website: beyondblue.org.au

**Mensline Australia**

Call: 1300 789 978

Website: mensline.org.au

**Standby Support After Suicide**

Call: 1300 727 247

Website: standbysupport.com.au

**Headspace**

Call: 1800 650 890

Website: headspace.org.au

# FOREWORD

Stories have the power to change lives.

Sometimes they do this quietly, through a familiar sentence, a moment of vulnerability that reminds us we are not alone, or a shared experience that gives us the courage to keep going when life feels overwhelming.

At Kintsugi Heroes, we believe deeply in the power of storytelling. Our mission is simple: to help people tell the stories they need to share so others can discover the stories they need to hear. Time and again, we see how sharing lived experience can create connection, reduce shame, and open the door to healing.

The Japanese philosophy of kintsugi teaches us that when something breaks, it can be repaired with gold, not to hide the cracks, but to honour them as part of the object's history. In many ways, our lives follow the same pattern. The moments that challenge us, the experiences that test us, and the struggles that shape us can become the very places where strength and wisdom are formed.

The story you are about to read is one of those journeys.

This book is a courageous and deeply personal reflection on the experience of Sarah, a mother navigating one of the most frightening moments a parent can face, supporting a child through a suicide attempt. It speaks honestly about fear, guilt, love, resilience, and the search for meaning in the midst of uncertainty.

What makes this story especially powerful is Sarah's willingness to transform pain into purpose. Through journalling, reflection, and the act of writing itself, Sarah has found a way not only to process her own experience but also to offer hope and understanding to others who may be walking a similar path.

Writing can be an extraordinary form of healing. When we place our thoughts and emotions on the page, we begin to see our experiences differently. The fragments of difficult moments can slowly come together, much like the gold seams of kintsugi, forming something that is not broken but beautifully human.

By sharing this story, Sarah has taken a brave step. Her words will undoubtedly resonate with parents, families, and individuals who have faced mental health struggles and wondered whether anyone else truly understands.

My hope is that readers of this book find comfort in its honesty, strength in its vulnerability, and reassurance that even in our most difficult moments, connection and hope remain possible.

Stories like this matter.

They remind us that none of us walks this path alone.

**Ian Westmoreland OAM**
Founder & CEO
Kintsugi Heroes

# FOREWORD

What happens to a mother's identity when the life she's built, protected, and believed in shifts in a single moment?

Not gradually. Not gently. But all at once.

This is the question that quietly runs beneath the surface of this book.

*So, Who Are You Anyway?* It is not simply a memoir about a crisis. It is an honest exploration of what it means to remain present in the middle of what you can't control, can't fix, and can't fully understand. It is a story of motherhood, grief, love, and the slow, often unseen work of making meaning after everything familiar has been disrupted.

But the foundation of this work is a thread that runs steadily throughout this book, one that I recognise deeply in my own work. It's the thread of language.

Language shapes the grief journey as it is lived.

Different words carry us into different places in different seasons. Words are never neutral. They accompany every thought, colour every experience, and quietly shape the way we receive, perceive, process, and believe what is happening in our lives. Words become the lens. They become the container. They become the anchor.

And anchors can do different things.

They can hold us in place. They can help us feel steady. They can also keep us tied to beliefs, fears, and stories that were never meant to define us. But healthy language, especially when explored through healthy writing and honest reflection, can begin to loosen what has been held too tightly. It can help us release what no longer serves us and receive what is needed now: awareness, possibility, compassion, meaning, hope.

Words give language to our experiences. They help us translate what has happened into something we can begin to understand. But when an experience goes unacknowledged, it does not simply disappear. It often settles into the inner life as fear, shame, doubt, confusion, or lack. It becomes a hidden narrative. And hidden narratives have a way of quietly shaping how we live until they are finally named.

This is one of the reasons writing matters so much.

Healthy writing and healthy reflection bring light to the unacknowledged experience. They create an opportunity to pause long enough to notice what has been hidden, what has gone unnamed, and what has been silently influencing how we think, feel, and move through the world. Writing weakens the power of what has remained buried by giving the writer a safe and honest place to see it, name it, and begin relating to it differently.

When I speak of healthy writing, I mean writing that helps produce a result aligned with the life you desire to create. I mean writing that does not simply circle pain but helps you witness it. Writing that gives your experience structure. Writing that offers enough space and steadiness for you to step back, observe your thoughts and language, and ask deeper questions that may lead to insight you could not access before.

That is what journalling can do.

Journalling gives the heart and mind space to meet ourselves where we are, even when we do not yet have all the words. Even the act of writing toward what cannot yet be spoken can cultivate safety. It reminds us that our voice is welcome, that our feelings are real, and that our lived experience is worthy of acknowledgment.

And as we learn to meet ourselves this way, with presence, validation, and compassion, we begin to grow in our capacity to offer that same kind of space to others.

This is why language work matters. This is why reflection matters. This is why writing matters.

As we learn to understand our thoughts, our emotions, and the impact of our words on our lives, we become more compassionate listeners. More thoughtful caregivers. More grounded leaders. More present coaches, healers, and helpers. We become people who know how to hold space for the truth of an experience without rushing to fix it.

That is part of what makes this book so meaningful.

The book you are about to read is a brave and courageous acknowledgment of Sarah's lived experience as a mother walking a road marked by grief, fear, love, uncertainty, and healing. She does not rush the story. She does not perform strength. She allows us to witness the process honestly, one word at a time.

*So, Who Are You Anyway?* is an invitation to slow down and meet ourselves exactly where we are, without the pressure of who we think we should be, need to be, or have to be. Sarah shows us, through her own story, that it is okay to give ourselves permission to tell the truth about our lives as they are. Not polished. Not wrapped up neatly. Just true.

She also offers something deeply generous through these pages. She shows how writing can become a companion through pain. How reflection can help us navigate thoughts, emotions, and language with more awareness. And how simple, accessible writing practices can support us in acknowledging our experiences in every season of life.

This book is for mothers and fathers. For writers, creatives, and storytellers. For helpers, healers, and space holders. For anyone who has known loss and love, grief and healing, suffering and peace. In other words, this book is for all of us living through the complexities of being human.

I believe these words will meet you where you are.

I believe they will offer companionship in places that may have felt lonely.

And I believe they may also give you a little more language for your own journey, along with a little more courage to keep moving forward one word at a time.

My hope is that you read this book with an open heart. That you allow its honesty to soften something in you. That you receive not only Sarah's story, but also the quiet invitation within it to acknowledge your own.

Sarah, thank you for sharing space with me in writing and for allowing your process to be seen. Thank you for the courage it takes to tell the truth about what you have lived. Thank you for honouring your story in a way that gives others permission to honour theirs too.

I salute you for your courage, your honesty, and your willingness to turn lived experience into language that can support someone else.

Wishing you every good thing for this book, for your words, and for all that grows from them.

**Nicole Annette**
Founder & CEO
The Journal Coaching Company

# FOREWORD

It is such an honour to be invited to contribute a few thoughts to the foreword of this book, on a subject that has been deeply meaningful to me throughout my life. I am humbled by the recognition from Sarah, and it is always insightful to see how someone responds to the personal way you choose to share your story.

For me, the art and act of journaling has always been a combination of creativity and processing. I am forever grateful for the notes I have written, because so often I don't remember those details when I look back. Journaling has allowed me to capture moments, emotions, and lessons that might otherwise have been lost.

In this work, the vulnerability Sarah shares is powerful and deeply connecting. It is truly inspiring. Like Sarah, my hope in sharing what I do—and what I have experienced—is to somehow span the space that can feel empty during dark times, to reach someone who needs to know they are not alone, and to offer very real, achievable solutions that have helped me. Sarah is doing just that. I sincerely applaud her for staying, fighting, and pushing through, even in the most difficult moments.

This book is a true reflection of the love in her heart—for her son, for herself, and for anyone she may reach.

Thank you for sharing this gift with the world.

**Heidi Swapp**
Designer, Paper Crafter, Entrepreneur, Memory Keeper and Suicide Prevention Advocate

# INTRODUCTION

*"I remain fascinated by where you go as a woman once you are a mother, and if you ever come back."*

**Rachel Cask**

The other day, I was talking to a friend about why it's completely normal for a parent to be emotional on their child's first day of school. Not just the very first day ever, but every year after a long holiday. With my youngest starting high school recently, I found myself wondering the usual things: Am I too sensitive? Too involved? Not relaxed enough? Too overprotective? And then I realised— it's perfectly okay to feel it all at once. Fear, relief, joy, celebration. To dismiss those feelings is to dismiss part of being a parent. That's what I call my 'mama heart', where all those messy, mixed emotions that show up repeatedly.

That truth was reinforced a few days later when I saw another mother in the school office, holding back tears. I asked if she was okay. "Year 9," she said. "I've got to get out of here before I cry." I smiled and replied, "It doesn't seem to get easier every year, does it?" In that moment, I knew my heart was right. I am okay. Simply fine, the way I am.

I wanted to write this story as a journey from brokenness to integration, where struggles are not hidden but highlighted as essential parts of who I have become. Writing from a lens of kintsugi, you see the cracks and follow along as I reflect and rebuild myself. This story is about embracing imperfection and, over time, revealing the gold of how my experiences have given me insight, strength and meaning to move forward.

There was a time when I believed that healing meant returning to 'normal' or to who I was before things fell apart. I know now that this was never the point. Like something once broken and carefully mended, my life carries its fractures openly. This is not the first time I have been fractured, but one of the most significant. One impacting my own son.

Each fracture, however, is a record of where I have been and how I have endured. This is not a story about fixing what was wrong; it is not about blaming or finding fault but learning to live within the visible seams. It is about discovering that those seams hold more strength and more beauty than what came before.

Over the past year or so, I've begun to regain some of my confidence. I notice the world with a sharper, closer eye. Colours seem brighter, moments feel fuller, and simply being present has become a gift. I am more observant, more aware, and more in tune with my own feelings. I can feel more deeply, notice the subtle shifts around me, and, importantly, set boundaries that protect my wellbeing.

But life has a way of shifting in a single moment, and I am not unaware of that either. Mine came on a day that started ordinarily but ended with my world tilting on the day I found out my then 16-year-old son had tried to take his own life. Nothing could have prepared me. Not scraped knees, not growing pains, not teenage tantrums. The fear, the silence, the ache — it was like stepping into a new life I never asked for.

This book is not about one moment in time. It is about everything that followed: the shock, the fear, the unanswered questions, and the slow, fragile return of hope. It is written for parents, for mothers who never imagined they would walk this path, and for anyone who has loved someone through mental ill health and found a way to keep going.

This is a story from my perspective as a mother. I have deliberately left out the perspective of other family members, as this is focused on my journey, but what I can share is that families do not survive grief because everyone feels the same thing at the same time. They survive because they continue to show up for one another, even when the paths through grief look different.

Despite how alone I felt throughout this experience, I largely made those choices, unconscious at times, myself, as I didn't have the words to reach out for help for myself straight away, and I didn't know how to speak to my loved ones about how I was feeling and how heartbroken I felt.

This experience has taught me that even within the same family, people carry pain differently. My husband and I each found our own ways of processing what had happened, sometimes speaking about it openly, and other times holding our thoughts more quietly. Staying connected through that uncertainty meant learning to respect those differences and trusting that love was still present, even when it was expressed in ways we didn't always recognise in the moment.

Life doesn't come unbroken. The cracks, the hard moments, the fears we carry are real, and they are ours. Journalling became my gold. Every word I wrote, every fear I named, every small victory I recorded, filled the cracks. It didn't erase the struggle, but it made the story stronger, more honest, more whole.

A little note about when writing about suicide and mental health, the language we use matters. Words can shape how readers understand an experience and whether they feel compassion or judgment. In recent years, many writers, clinicians, and advocacy groups have encouraged the use of language that is respectful, accurate, and centred on the person rather than the act. Organisations such as Mindframe National Media Initiative and the World Health Organisation recommend wording that reduces stigma and reflects the humanity of those involved.

For this reason, many people now use phrases such as *'died by suicide,' 'attempted suicide,' or 'survived a suicide attempt.'* In more personal storytelling, such as this book, it can also feel natural to write that someone *'tried to end their life'* or that they were *'struggling deeply with their mental health.'* These expressions describe what happened without suggesting blame, failure, or wrongdoing. They allow the focus to remain on the individual and their experience, rather than defining them by the act itself.

Some older expressions are increasingly avoided because of the meanings they can unintentionally carry. The phrase *'committed suicide,'* for example, has historical associations with crime or sin, while terms like *'failed attempt'* or *'successful suicide'* can imply that death is a success and survival is a failure. For many people affected by suicide, these words can feel harsh or stigmatising, even when they are used without that intention.

Another important consideration is person-first language. Rather than describing someone simply as *'mentally ill,'* you may find many writers prefer to say that a person is *'living with mental illness'* or *'experiencing depression.'* Conditions such as depression or bipolar disorder may be named when they are part of the story, but they do not define the whole person. This approach acknowledges the reality of mental illness while still recognising the complexity, dignity, and individuality of each life.

Ultimately, the goal of using thoughtful language is not to soften the truth, but to speak about difficult experiences with care. When stories about suicide and mental health are told with compassion and respect, they can help reduce stigma, foster understanding, and remind readers that behind every story is a human being who deserves empathy.

At its heart, this book is a love story about a mother's love tested, stretched, and reshaped by survival. It has allowed me to reflect on myself, my children, and the unspoken truths we carry. Even years later, it can still be hard to talk about, which is exactly why I am sharing it.

***Dear My Beautiful Boy,***

*There are things I didn't see.*

*And there are things I still don't fully understand.*

*If I could go back, I would study your silences more closely. I would sit longer in your room.*

*I would ask different questions.*

*But this story isn't about blame.*

*It's about love. And survival. And the quiet ways we try to hold each other together.*

*You have always been thoughtful. Sensitive. Deep feeling in ways that don't always fit comfortably in this world.*

*I thought I was raising you to be strong.*

*I didn't realise how heavy strength can feel when you're carrying it alone.*

*This book is not about what you did.*

*It is about how fiercely you are loved.*

*Always,*

*Mum*

This is not a how-to manual, and it doesn't offer easy answers. It is a lived experience—messy, emotional, honest and written for those who need to know that what they feel is human. That it is not your fault, and you haven't done anything wrong. I do share some resources I've found helpful, and the ways I've worked through my thoughts, but the focus here is on experience, not instruction.

My son is alive. Those words carry both gratitude and responsibility. Grateful that he is here. Responsibility to speak openly about what it took to get here, and what continues to be learned along the way.

The day my son tried to end his life is burned into my memory. Time seemed to stop, yet everything collapsed at once. As a mother, I had always believed my role was to protect him, to guide him safely through life's storms. But nothing could have prepared me for the moment I realised I couldn't shield him from his own pain.

I remember how heavy it felt. Not just emotionally, but physically, as if my chest was carrying a weight, it was never meant to hold. I moved into immediate response mode, as I have done countless times in my career, to support clients or staff. And yet, shame wrapped around me, keeping me silent and isolated. I felt like I was drowning in fear and heartbreak while the world carried on unchanged.

Questions circled endlessly: How did we get here? What did I miss? How do we go on? There were no easy answers—only an ache that settled in my chest and a fear that followed me everywhere.

Looking back, I can see that in those early days, I was reaching for anything that might help me survive the weight of it all. I needed a place to put what I was carrying, somewhere my fear, confusion, and grief could exist without needing to be solved.

I began to write. Not with purpose or plan, but simply as a way to keep breathing. My words were often fragmented, unfinished, reflecting how I felt inside. I wasn't trying to make sense of what had happened; I was trying to endure it.

Writing didn't change what my son was going through. It didn't remove the uncertainty. But it gave me a way to stay present. It created a quiet space for honesty, where sorrow, anger, and fragile hope could exist side by side. Over time, those words became something I could lean on, even when everything else felt unsteady.

Some sections of this book may be confronting. The intention is to share my perspective only, not to criticise or instruct. Please read at your own pace and seek support if you need it.

If you are reading this as a parent, carer, or loved one who has walked a similar path, I hope these pages remind you that your reactions, fear, anger, exhaustion and your love are human. If you are reading to better understand, I hope this story offers insight into the complexity of survival and the strength it takes to keep going, for both parent and child.

I also hope it shows how a child's experience can lead to deep reflection, opening space for shifts in perspective and new priorities. For me, it has led to a focus on mental wellbeing, not just for my children, but for myself, and a clearer sense of what I need from the world.

So, what led me to write this book? I always dreamed of writing, though I never imagined a narrative nonfiction memoir would be on the cards. Journalling began as a coping mechanism, a container to hold my feelings, a place for thoughts I could not express to anyone else. It was cathartic, and over time it became something more: a way to reflect, process, and survive.

On any given day, I was balancing a professional career, motherhood, and my role as a wife. As my children have grown, I've learned to move between these roles with a kind of quiet adaptability, responding to what was needed most in each moment. I once read the quote, 'Hope is not a strategy,' and while that may be true, there were days when hope was the only thing I had to hold onto.

I also realised there are many others who have walked similar paths and have shown resilience, who have survived, and continued to navigate the ongoing challenges of mental health. I wanted to share our journey so families and caregivers might believe in hope together. We are not alone, even when it feels like it. Mental health can be talked about without shame.

As Sarah Martin writes in her book *Dear Psychosis,* mental illness is silent and often invisible because people are reluctant to speak up for themselves or their loved ones, fearing judgment or repercussions. This is a story about staying and holding on when certainty disappears. About finding a way forward, one careful step at a time.

CHAPTER ONE

# THE ROOTS OF MOTHERHOOD

Motherhood begins long before a child arrives. It begins in the ways we see the world, the habits we carry, and the quiet lessons we absorb along the way. I have always been someone who notices the details, such as the rhythms of daily life, the small gestures of care, and the moments that often go unseen. Over time, I learned that love is rarely loud or dramatic. It shows up in steady presence, patience, attentiveness, and the subtle ways we hold space for those we care about.

I grew up in a household shaped by clearly defined traditional roles, where my mother cared for the home and children, and my father worked outside the home and handled external responsibilities. I learned early on the value of independence, observation, and quiet resilience. I watched closely, noticed what was needed, and stepped in where I could, habits that became second nature to me.

In GG Renee Hill's book, *Story Work,* she describes how our families influence us: the joy, the pain, the gifts and the traditions are passed down through the generations. Hill explains that families are full of flawed beings who give us habits, coping mechanisms and tools for living, some by direction and some by example. I have thought long and hard about what this means for my children, and for me. Sometimes we do accept these birthrights without questioning them, says Hill, even when they do not serve us moving forward.

While these early experiences shaped who I am, they also clarified what I wanted to do differently. I didn't want to recreate that same structure in my own home. Instead, I was drawn toward a way of living that felt more open, more shared and grounded in partnership, communication, and mutual growth. It wasn't something I had often seen modelled, but I felt strongly called to create it for myself and my family.

In my adult life, I embraced this vision intentionally. One example that comes to mind is representing a feminist group at university, exploring ideas of equality, collaboration, and honesty in relationships. These principles carried forward into the way I approached parenting.

GG Renee Hill also says that, through generations, the family's identity evolves through the stories passed down, forged from the memories and imaginations of its members. I have always wanted to embrace this, to walk alongside my children, to be honest with them, to share life's journey openly, and to remain available to talk about anything. I aim to guide them while giving them the freedom to explore, make mistakes, and learn for themselves.

In many ways, our household doesn't follow the traditional model I grew up with. But this wasn't something we sat down and deliberately planned, but it unfolded over time, shaped by circumstance as much as intention.

With my husband travelling significant distances for work each day, much of the rhythm of our home naturally fell to me. I have had the flexibility of working from home. The day-to-day logistics, the emotional pulse of the household, and the constant adjustments that come with raising children became my space to hold. Not out of expectation, but out of necessity.

And yet, within that, something different began to take shape.

While the structure of our roles may have appeared traditional from the outside, the values underneath were not. There is an ongoing sense of partnership, of shared responsibility, even if it didn't always look equal in time or presence. When he was home, my husband was usually busy with household tasks. When decisions needed to be made, they were ours, not mine alone.

I began to understand that redefining gender roles isn't always about rejecting them entirely. Sometimes, it's about quietly reshaping them, allowing flexibility, understanding, and communication to replace rigid expectations.

Sometimes I carried more than I thought I could. There may be points throughout this book when the imbalance feels heavy. This is largely because I didn't allow myself to share my feelings and thoughts with anyone. I sat on them, often describing myself as alone. But there were, and continue to be, moments of strength, of growth, and of deep connection with my children, with myself, and within our marriage.

What I have come to see is that motherhood does not exist in a fixed structure. It adapts. It responds. It evolves alongside the realities of life.

And in that evolution, I found my own way, one that honours both the demands placed upon me and the values I have chosen to live by.

Even as I embraced my role as the primary caregiver, I became acutely aware that much of the emotional load rested with me. Balancing care, attention, and guidance while keeping family life steady was a responsibility I carried deeply. At the same time, I moved through it with intention, drawing on what I had cultivated over many years: patience, presence, attentiveness, and openness. I wanted to create an environment where my children felt supported, seen, and free to explore, even as I carried the weight of making sure everything held together.

Over time, I also came to recognise that the way I parent differs from that of some others. It is more relaxed, rooted in partnership rather than control. I strive for honesty and openness, valuing dialogue and a shared sense of clarity. I want my children to see the world clearly, ask questions, and engage fully with life, knowing they have a trusted adult who will listen, stand beside them, and guide them without imposing rigid rules. At the heart of this way of parenting are curiosity, empathy, and a steady attentiveness, shaped by observation, reflection, and the choices I have made along the way.

The experience of supporting my son's mental health journey, however, has made me question everything I thought I knew about being a parent.

*Have I not been fit enough to lead, support, and raise two boys in the context of what has happened?* The sense of helplessness and deep sadness shook me to my absolute core. *Have I ever been a 'good' mum? Will I ever have the confidence again to be the mother they need?*

I remember my own mother once telling me that the very fact that I worry about this and ask myself those questions makes me a 'good mum'. I am not so sure.

Looking back, I can see how these roots shaped the parent I became, at least at one time. The patience, resilience, and steady attentiveness I developed over years of reflection became the foundation for navigating the unexpected, the difficult, and the moments that tested me in ways I could never have imagined. Understanding where I came from, along with my values, my instincts, and my way of seeing and processing the world, offers insight into how I met my children with love, presence, and care.

Even now, I recognise that parenting is a continuous process of learning and adaptation, and at times I feel as though I still know nothing. The principles I carry, openness, partnership, honesty, and a way of paying close attention, act as a compass, guiding me through ordinary days and unexpected storms alike. They shape a space where love is active, present, and unafraid of life's complexities, and they remind me that motherhood is as much about growth as it is about care.

I wanted to be that mum who turns up the music loud and dances around the house. I wanted to be a mother who takes care of herself, setting an example for my children. I wanted to be the kind of mum who lets kids be kids, to jump in puddles, build tent forts. I wanted my children to express their feelings and dreams; to know they could call me at any time, day or night, and I would be there for them.

I hope to walk alongside them while also giving them space to explore, make mistakes, and learn for themselves. This way of parenting reflects what I absorbed over a lifetime: patience, presence, curiosity, and the understanding that love is best expressed through care, openness, and mutual respect rather than rules alone.

I have also come to understand that the way I parent is shaped not only by what I experienced, but by observing the subtle ways people respond to life, the balance of strength and gentleness, the courage it takes to navigate challenges without losing sight of what matters.

***Dear Younger Me,***

*You are trying so hard to do this differently.*

*You believe awareness will protect you.*

*You believe love will be enough.*

*You believe strength means carrying it all without asking for help.*

*It won't always work that way.*

*You will become the steady one. The capable one. The one who holds the emotions, the logistics, the silence.*

*And when the night comes that shakes everything, you will search yourself for what you missed.*

*Listen carefully:*

*You did not fail.*

*You loved.*

*You showed up.*

*You stayed.*

*Strength is not doing it alone.*

*And motherhood is not measured by preventing pain.*

*Be softer with yourself.*

*You are not the reason this happened.*

*You are the reason he was not alone.*

— *You*

One of the unexpected lessons this journey has given me is the clarity to see our values, both as individuals and as a family. I have learned to notice not just what we believe, but why we believe it, and how that shapes the way we show up for each other.

Sometimes, those values feel very different from what I grew up with. While my family of origin may have emphasised control, achievement, or appearances, I find myself drawn to presence, patience, and emotional honesty. Where they avoided uncomfortable conversations, I have learned to lean into them, to sit with uncertainty, and to name what is real, even when it is messy or painful.

I do not frame these differences as 'right' or 'wrong.' They are simply different, and that awareness has brought me a kind of wisdom I could not have gained any other way. I see now that understanding these contrasts is not about criticising my family or their choices, but about recognising the patterns I want to continue or change in my own life.

It has taught me that values are living things. They are shaped by experience, by reflection, and by love. They guide how we parent, how we support one another, and how we respond to the world around us.

Most importantly, this reflection has shown me that it is possible for us to honour both where we came from and who we are becoming. To take the parts of our upbringing that serve us, and to consciously shape the parts that don't, with compassion and without judgement.

As I grew into adulthood and then into motherhood, I began to see that being different was not a weakness. It was a choice to parent with openness, empathy, and awareness, the qualities I had longed for in my own childhood. I realised that toughness, demonstrating hard work and resilience, doesn't have to look a certain way, and strength isn't measured by endurance alone.

I have often felt like the black sheep in my family, and that difference has shaped the way I choose to parent. I strive to be authentic, to embrace emotional honesty, and to create a home where feelings can exist safely alongside the everyday challenges of life. This looks like open conversations around the dinner table, inviting my children's views and feedback, and both parents being fully present at milestones and significant moments. Choosing this path, so different from my own upbringing, has given me a sense of freedom and a deeper connection to my children and to myself, even in the face of criticism from those closest to me.

In parenting, marriage, and in life, this awareness becomes a quiet compass. It helps me navigate the moments of fear, the moments of joy, and the moments when nothing feels certain, and reminds me that what matters most is the love and intention we bring to each day.

I hope you will hear through the story to come that I now pay closer attention to the rhythms of emotion, to the unspoken needs of those around me, and to the ways patience and understanding can shape relationships. These insights guide my decisions as a mother, helping me offer both freedom and support, honesty and empathy, structure and flexibility.

I want to be the mother who goes on adventures, but not in competition with anyone (even myself!). I want to make decisions out of love, not to one-up anyone or post a better photo at the end of the day. And to serve alongside my children, volunteering and modelling what life can look like when giving to others and bringing joy to the world.

I can now see how these roots shaped the mother I became and who I will be moving forward. The patience, resilience, and quiet attentiveness I developed over years of observation and reflection became the foundation for facing the unexpected, the difficult, and the moments that tested me in ways I could never have imagined. Understanding where I came from and how my values, my instincts, and the way I see and process the world offer insight into my approach to motherhood and to meeting my children with love, presence, and care.

Even now, I recognise that parenting is never perfect, and I need to be kinder to myself. It is a journey of constant learning, adjustment, and reflection. But the foundation I built, the lessons I carried, and my principles of openness, partnership, patience, and honesty have given me a compass. They guide me through both ordinary days and unexpected storms, shaping a space where love is active, present, and unafraid of life's complexities.

I want to be the mother who teaches my boys that loving those in our household means everything, and who builds a life moving forward that is peaceful and that my family will remember fondly. I want my husband and I to continue building a home that is a safe place for my boys to be themselves, find freedom, and return to at any time.

Most importantly, though, I want to continue to be the mother who forgives quickly and asks forgiveness when I am not doing so well, and to be the mother whose boys know I love them and am on their team, no matter what, until the day I die.

As I look back on these early lessons and the values I carried into motherhood, I can see how they prepared me for the unexpected, the challenging, and the profoundly meaningful moments that were still to come. I could not have known then how deeply those roots would be tested, how my patience, presence, and openness would be called upon in ways I never imagined. Yet it was these very foundations of observation, reflection, care, and a commitment to honest, open relationships that would guide me through the journey ahead, shaping not only the mother I became but also the connection I would forge with my children in the face of life's uncertainties.

CHAPTER TWO

# THE DAY EVERYTHING CHANGED

No parent imagines the exact path their child will take, or the challenges that may arise along the way. I entered motherhood with values, intentions, and hopes shaped by my own life—honesty, openness, presence, and partnership—but life has a way of testing even the best-laid plans.

My son's journey brought lessons I could never have anticipated. It challenged my patience, stretched my understanding of love, and revealed the depths of resilience that both parent and child must find. There were times of uncertainty or when fear and doubt crept in, and moments when I questioned whether I was doing enough, saying the right words, or holding the space he needed. Yet through it all, I discovered that parenting is not about having all the answers; it is about presence, attention, and the willingness to walk beside your child, even in the most difficult moments.

This story is not just about struggles or hardships; it is about connection, insight, and the quiet resilience that grows when a parent and child navigate life together. It reflects learning to trust, to listen, and to meet each challenge with care, honesty, and openness. It is also about the ways our shared experiences deepen understanding, foster growth, and create the bonds that carry us through both ordinary days and extraordinary trials.

Through every uncertainty, the foundations I carried, the lessons from my own roots, and the value of observation, reflection, and thoughtful care became essential. They reminded me that parenting is both a challenge and a privilege, a journey of growth for both child and parent, and an opportunity to put the values I hold most dearly into practice, even when the path is unpredictable.

It was the 19th of October 2023 — a perfectly ordinary day. The morning routine had been uneventful. I was working from home, conducting interviews with a colleague, when I decided to take a short lunch break and run to the local supermarket.

When I got back, the first thing I noticed was the kitchen bench. Tablets and pill packets were scattered everywhere, some overturned, some empty. My stomach dropped. Something had gone terribly wrong.

I ran straight to my son's room. He was lying there, still and heavy against the mattress. It didn't take long for me to see that he had taken the pills. I moved closer, checking that he was breathing, trying to gauge his responsiveness.

Fear and disbelief hit me like a wave. I screamed. My voice seemed impossibly loud in the quiet room. He sat up abruptly, pacing, crying and saying over and over, "I'm sorry. I'm sorry. I'm sorry."

I asked him, "What have you done?" My voice shook, though I tried to keep it steady, reassuring. Then I went into automatic mode. I called the ambulance and followed their instructions to the letter. At the same time, I rang a friend to pick up my younger son from school.

Eventually, he lay back down on the bed, waiting quietly. His speech was slurred, his skin damp with sweat. I stayed close, keeping him talking in low, steady tones, trying to follow every word the operator said. The scattered medication packets on the bench were a stark reminder of how quickly life can change.

I couldn't believe it had happened so fast. If only I'd been home, maybe none of this would have happened.

The ambulance arrived faster than I expected, though the minutes felt like hours. Paramedics attended (I don't even remember them arriving) moved quickly, calmly assessing him, checking his vitals, and preparing him for the ride to the hospital. I stayed close, holding his hand, murmuring small reassurances, trying to keep my own panic from spilling over.

As they worked, my mind raced. *How had it come to this? Had I missed something? Could I have done more?* The questions spun endlessly, but there were no easy answers, only the sharp ache of fear and the need to act.

Once he was safely in their care, I sat on the edge of the bed, trying to catch my breath. Everything felt surreal — the ordinary morning, the lunch break, and then this sudden rupture in the rhythm of life. I kept thinking that we were supposed to be okay. And yet, here we were, facing a reality I never imagined.

Through it all, I tried to hold onto one thing: presence. My job in that moment wasn't to understand or fix anything. It was to be there, fully, for my son, for the fragile space between panic and relief. To stay steady, to witness, and to ensure he knew he wasn't alone. I had done this many times in my professional life as I dealt with staff who found deceased clients and emergency situations…

I slipped into automatic mode. The first thing I did was call my husband, letting him know what had happened and arranging for our younger son to be picked up from school. I messaged my colleague to let her know I wouldn't make the last scheduled interview. Even amid the panic, there was a strange rhythm to it all — coordinating, calling, checking, and making sure that everyone and everything around me was in place.

I don't remember much of the drive to the hospital. I had to wait for my younger son to be dropped off at home first, and the time in between feels almost like a blur now. Everything was moving so fast, yet in slow motion. The fear, the adrenaline, the worry for my son meant that I barely noticed the passing streets. I just remember holding onto the thought that he needed me, and that I had to stay present, no matter how hard it felt.

By the time we arrived, he was still in the ambulance bay, waiting quietly with his eyes closed. Things weren't rushed; the staff moved with steady calm, but they kept a close eye on him, monitoring his vitals and ensuring he could rest safely. I stayed seated at the foot of the trolley, feeling the tension slowly ease just a little, grateful for the quiet efficiency around us and trying to keep my own racing thoughts in check.

One of the paramedics occupied my younger son with a conversation about the latest Pokémon game and various character details. I tried to smile as I listened to their conversation and added comments where appropriate to keep it sounding like an everyday chat.

Medical staff documented the incident as described by the paramedics, recording what he had ingested and the time of ingestion. They explained the monitoring process and what to expect in the coming hours and seemed happy for him to sleep while they awaited blood test results.

I remember sitting there and listening. It felt like an out-of-body experience, as if I were observing us or talking to a client. This, however, was MY SON. Who was seemingly void of feeling, emotion, and void of any realisation that from today, life had changed forever.

Earlier in the month, we enjoyed a family weekend away with friends; my son was learning to drive, working with a personal trainer, and playing in the State Netball Titles. Life seemed good.

I remember we waited many hours for a bed and the next steps. I remember how tiring the hospital questions became. The first time felt reasonable. Someone needed to know what had happened, and I was grateful that they were listening.

At triage, the paramedics told the story carefully. I added information to get the timeline right: when things started, what I noticed first, and what had changed. The nurse nodded and typed as I spoke. When I finished, I felt a small sense of relief. At least now someone understood.

But a little while later, another nurse appeared beside the bed.

"What's been happening today?"

So, I began again.

I told the same story, trying to keep the details consistent and not forget anything important. By the time I finished, I was already feeling the heaviness of it. Hospitals are tiring places even when nothing is wrong. When you're worried, when you're holding fear just under the surface, the effort of explaining everything again felt overwhelming.

There is a particular kind of exhaustion that comes from repeating the same story. At the hospital, each new face meant starting again; explaining what had happened, retracing the details, finding the words for something that still didn't make sense to me. Doctor after doctor, nurse after nurse, each conversation necessary, every question important, and yet each one asking me to reopen something that was still raw.

I found myself repeating the same sentences, almost mechanically at times, as if saying it often enough might make it feel more real, or somehow easier to carry. But it didn't. With every retelling came a quiet depletion: emotional, mental, even physical. By the end, I wasn't just tired from the situation itself, but from the weight of having to hold it, explain it, and relive it again. It was a different kind of fatigue, one that settled deep within me, where words no longer felt like enough, but silence wasn't an option either.

Then the next doctor arrived.

"Can you tell me what's been going on?"

Again, I began from the beginning.

The timeline. The symptoms. The small details I was afraid to leave out in case they mattered. I watched their pen move across the paper as I spoke. I wondered if I was saying it the same way as before. I wondered if I had forgotten something.

Hours passed, and the story travelled through the hospital like a baton in a relay race. Another doctor. Another nurse. A registrar checking in. Each time, the same questions, gently asked, carefully recorded.

"Has this happened before? What medications are you taking?"

Each time I went back to the beginning.

By the end, the story didn't feel like my story anymore. It felt rehearsed, worn thin from being told too many times. I could hear myself repeating the words almost automatically, as though I had stepped outside the experience and was simply reciting the script.

Later, I understood that every person needed to hear it for themselves. It was part of the system, part of making sure nothing was missed. But in that moment, it felt strangely lonely, as I repeated the same story, hoping that this time it would be the last time I had to say it out loud.

It often made me wonder what happens to the people who don't have someone by their side through this? Someone to speak when they can't, to remember details when everything feels blurred, to advocate when the system feels overwhelming. The hospital process requires clarity, repetition, and a kind of emotional stamina that feels almost impossible in those moments.

I found myself holding pieces together simply because I had to, but I was not the one in crisis. For those who walk into that space alone, already carrying so much, I can only imagine how heavy it must feel. *How do they find the words? How do they keep going through each question, each explanation, each decision?* It brought a quiet awareness to me of how vital support is in those moments, not just clinical care, but human presence. Someone sitting beside you saying, "I'm here. You don't have to do this alone."

It highlighted for me just how important advocacy is within the mental health system. Not everyone has the capacity to ask questions, challenge decisions, or even fully understand what is being said during a crisis. A support person, whether a parent, partner, friend, or carer, can become a vital bridge between the individual and the systems around them. They can listen when details are missed, speak up when something doesn't feel right, and help ensure that care is not only delivered, but understood.

Advocacy is not about taking over; it is about standing alongside someone when they feel most vulnerable. It is about helping their voice be heard when it feels too hard to speak and reminding them, and sometimes the system, that behind every assessment, every form, and every question, there is a person who needs compassion, patience, and to be truly seen.

In between awaiting test results for my son, travelling to and from home and then returning to the hospital, we finally got to see a psychiatrist for assessment to determine the next steps. Once again, we outlined what had happened.

Despite the cubicle curtain being drawn, it felt like there was no privacy (we all know how anti-soundproof they are). The psychiatrist spoke calmly, asking questions to gauge my son's state of mind, his thoughts leading up to the attempt, and his emotional response since.

I sat beside him, listening, my hands tightly clasped in my lap, my chest heavy, trying not to cry. The air felt thick with silence, punctuated only by his quiet words and the psychiatrist's soft voice. Every answer, every pause, I found I was holding out for hope. Whilst the intent was clearly to end his life, there was no recognition that he was pleased he did not complete this.

I remember the shock of it—the surrealness of watching someone so familiar, so deeply my own child, speak as if he were a stranger providing answers I did not want to hear. And yet, I was there, present, trying to absorb, to support, to respond, but feeling, deep down, that the world had shifted irreversibly in that room, in that moment.

Knowing that the anchor points in his life were his brother, his dog, and his friends and family was a pleasure to my ears. My son could recognise who missed him. This did not change his emotional state, though, but was something I had expected. I was waiting for the tears, outpouring of grief…something…but nothing came.

The psychiatric assessment ended, and the psychiatrist asked if he wanted to be admitted to the hospital or to go home. I felt the room tighten around me as we considered the options. *How could a young person make this decision?*

Knowing what I knew about the mental health service, the horror stories I had heard and lived through various clients over time, home was the only option. It was the place where he was safest, where I could provide the vigilance and care he needed. I quietly accepted the reality that the responsibility for his immediate safety rested entirely on me.

When we eventually left the hospital, it was the early morning of the next day. It was chilly, and we were both shaking, our teeth chattering as we got to the car, without a jumper or any thought of bringing clothing to keep us warm. I didn't really know what to say. I thought he might be hungry, so we got a bite to eat at McDonald's on the way home.

Sitting beside him in the car, a heavy, quiet exhaustion pressed down on me, as though every part of my body had been carrying the weight of the day. Every detail, the scattered pills, the screaming, the relentless hum of hospital monitors, was etched into my mind, impossible to ignore or erase. I felt hollow, drained, and yet hyper-aware: acutely conscious of the fragility of life, the fine line we had just crossed, and the reality that nothing would ever feel quite the same again.

Relief flickered through me in moments, only to be replaced by a gnawing fear that it could happen again, a vigilance I could neither switch off nor escape. In that quiet, cramped car, I felt the paradox of motherhood at its rawest: utterly exhausted, yet utterly present, carrying both grief and hope in the same breath.

The drive home was heavy with silence. My son stared out the window, expressionless, as I gripped the steering wheel tightly. Each turn, each stoplight, each familiar street felt like a reminder that the day had shifted everything, forever.

We both went off to bed long after my husband and younger son had fallen asleep. I can't recall sleeping much that night. I lie in bed, silently, feeling the weight of the day, the fear, the relief, and the impossibility of returning to 'normal' ever again. I have never felt so alone.

Though the immediate crisis had been managed, the responsibility for his safety, his healing, and his emotional wellbeing rested solely with me. I knew the long hours ahead, the conversations, the vigilance, the care would sit with me, within my heart.

***Dear My Beautiful Boy,***

*That night in the curtained cubicle, close to midnight, I watched you answer questions in a voice I barely recognised. You sounded distant, as if you were speaking from somewhere far away — somewhere I couldn't quite reach.*

*I sat beside you, close enough to touch, but it felt like there was an ocean between us.*

*You kept your answers short. Careful. Contained. And I wondered how much you were holding inside — how much pain you had been carrying without letting me see.*

*I wanted to gather it all from you. I wanted to take the heaviness and carry it myself.*

*You thought you were a burden.*

*You thought we would be better without you.*

*But you have always been my heart walking around outside my body.*

*That night, even in the harsh hospital light, even in the silence between your words, I saw the same boy who once held my hand crossing the road, who laughed too loudly at silly jokes, who slept curled on his side as a little boy.*

*Nothing — not this night, not your despair, not your confusion — could ever make you less loved.*

*I wish you could see yourself the way I do.*

*Love always,*

*Mum*

CHAPTER THREE

# THE GRIEF WE CAN NAME, AND THE GRIEF WE CANNOT

In 2012, I lost a baby. Our son was born still.

There are moments in life that divide time into before and after. Losing our baby was one of those moments. The silence in the room where there should have been crying was something I will never forget. As a mother, every instinct in my body had prepared me to protect, nurture, and welcome him into the world. Instead, I was left holding a grief that had nowhere to go.

The world, however, understands this kind of loss. People knew what to say, even if the words were imperfect. They brought flowers and sent messages. They acknowledged that something sacred had been broken. There were rituals for grief: burial arrangements, condolences, quiet understanding. The pain was unbearable, but it was recognised.

Losing our baby changed me. It changed the way I saw life, the way I held my children, and the way I understood fragility. It also tested my marriage in ways I hadn't anticipated – in all the right ways, bringing us closer and sharing in the pain together. Grief has a way of moving differently through two people who love each other deeply. Sometimes we leaned into each other. At other times, we stood quietly beside one another, each carrying something too heavy to fully explain.

Years later, when our oldest son tried to take his own life, I experienced another moment that divided life into before and after. My husband experienced this differently, too, and had his own ways of working through and interpreting the events that had occurred.

But this grief was different.

This time, my teenager was still here. He was breathing, alive, present in the world. And yet the fear, the shock, and the heartbreak ran just as deep. It was a grief born not of death, but of the possibility of losing him. Of realising that the pain inside someone you love had grown so large that they could no longer see a way through it.

What struck me most was how differently the world responds to these two experiences.

When a baby dies, the community gathers around you. People recognise the tragedy. They speak gently. They acknowledge the loss.

When a teenager struggles with mental illness or attempts suicide, the silence can be overwhelming. Conversations become hesitant. Some people don't know what to say, and others avoid the topic altogether. The grief becomes private, hidden, and sometimes wrapped in shame.

As a mother, both experiences touched the same sacred place in my heart—the instinct to protect my son and the devastation of realising that sometimes we cannot shield them from pain.

The grief of losing a baby is often acknowledged, visible, and even spoken of openly by those around you. But the grief of living through a teenager's mental health crisis is quieter, shadowed, and largely unseen. It creeps into everyday life in ways that are subtle yet relentless — the sleepless nights, the moments of panic, the constant recalibration of hope and fear.

It was an unfamiliar, complicated grief that I struggled to name, and which has taken me years to process. Nothing had been lost in the traditional sense. My son was still here. And yet something inside me had shifted, and with it came a quiet mourning for the life I thought we were living before that moment.

Both forms of grief reshape a family, shifting how you see the world, how you hold your loved ones, and how you come to understand what truly matters in life.

It stirred up old feelings I had tried to put aside for years. Past criticisms I had carried about myself began to surface again, whispering doubts that I thought I had already made peace with. I questioned my choices, my parenting, the way I had shown up in the world. In quiet moments, I found myself wondering if I had missed something important, if I had somehow failed to see what was right in front of me.

Alongside that came the weight of relationships that had fractured over time. Family misunderstandings. Friendships that had faded or broken under pressure. During such a vulnerable moment, those absences felt louder than ever. I found myself wishing for conversations that had never happened, for support that had not always been there, and for connections that had once felt solid but were no longer within reach.

What surprised me most was the helplessness. As parents, we spend so much of our lives believing that we can protect our children, guide them, shield them from the worst parts of the world. But in that moment, I realised there are things no parent can control. Mental pain is invisible, complex, and deeply personal. No amount of love can completely guard against it.

That helplessness was painful to sit with. It forced me to confront the limits of what I could do, and the uncomfortable truth that sometimes we can only stand beside someone we love while they walk through their own darkness.

And yet, within that grief, there was also a quiet shift in understanding. I began to see that grief does not only belong to loss through death. It can also emerge when our sense of certainty collapses, when the story we believed about our lives changes suddenly and without warning.

This was grief for the life I thought we had. Grief for the illusion that love alone could protect those we care about. And perhaps, in some ways, grief for parts of myself that I was now being asked to rediscover with more compassion and honesty.

There is a kind of grief that rarely gets spoken about when someone survives a suicide attempt. It is quiet, complicated, and difficult to explain. From the outside, people often respond with relief—thank goodness they're still here. And that relief is real. It is powerful. But alongside it sits another emotion that is harder to name.

Grief.

It feels strange to admit grief when the person you love is still alive. There has been no funeral, no formal moment where the world pauses to acknowledge what has happened. Life seems to continue around you as if everything has returned to normal. But inside the family, something has shifted. The ground beneath you feels different.

For parents, siblings, and loved ones, there can be a quiet mourning for the innocence that existed before the attempt. Before the moment when you realised just how much pain someone you love was carrying. Before the terrifying understanding that life can become fragile in ways you never imagined.

You may grieve the certainty you once had. The belief that love alone could protect the people closest to you. The sense of safety you felt in your family's story. After a suicide attempt, those things can feel altered, as though the world has revealed a vulnerability that cannot be unseen.

There can also be grief for the version of your loved one you thought you knew. Not because they have changed completely, but because you now understand that there were parts of their struggle that were invisible to you. That realisation can be painful, leaving you wondering what you might have missed, what conversations might have helped, or whether things could have been different.

Siblings often carry this quietly. They may feel fear, confusion, anger, or protectiveness, but struggle to find space to speak about it. Parents can feel an overwhelming mixture of relief and guilt. Relief that their child survived, and guilt for questions that have no clear answers. Everyone in the family can find themselves holding emotions that do not fit neatly into the ways we usually talk about grief.

Yet this kind of grief also deserves recognition. It is the grief of having seen how close you came to losing someone. Understanding that mental pain can run deeper than anyone realised. It is the grief of standing in the space between relief and heartbreak, trying to make sense of both at once.

Acknowledging this quiet grief does not take away from the hope of recovery. Instead, it allows families to be honest about the emotional impact of the experience. Healing, after all, does not only belong to the person who attempted to end their life. It belongs to the whole family who walked through that moment with them, carrying their own silent burdens along the way.

Journalling can be a powerful way to process grief because it allows feelings to surface in a private, honest space without judgment. When grief is complicated—especially after experiences involving mental ill health or trauma—it can be difficult to speak openly about emotions. Writing can offer a gentle way to untangle those feelings and give them shape. Over time, journalling can help people understand their grief, honour their experiences, and find meaning in what they have lived through.

***Dear Grief,***

*You arrived quietly at first. I did not recognise you straight away. You slipped into ordinary moments and sat beside me in places I never expected—at the kitchen table, in the car, in the stillness of the night when everything else had gone quiet. I tried, for a long time, to push you away. I thought if I ignored you long enough, you might leave.*

*But you stayed.*

*At first, I resented you. You carried questions I could not answer and emotions I did not want to feel. You reminded me of things that had changed, things that could never quite return to the way they were before. You forced me to sit with uncertainty and helplessness—two things I had spent most of my life trying to avoid.*

*Yet over time, something shifted.*

*You began to teach me.*

*You taught me that love is deeper and more complicated than I once understood. That, when we love someone fiercely, we also become vulnerable to pain we cannot control. You showed me that strength does not always look like fixing things. Sometimes it looks like sitting beside someone you care about, even when you cannot make their suffering disappear.*

*You also taught me compassion—both for others and for myself. Before you arrived, I was often quick to judge my own mistakes and perceived shortcomings. But grief softened something in me. It reminded me that we are all human, all imperfect, all carrying stories that others may never fully see.*

*Perhaps most importantly, you taught me that life rarely follows the neat path we imagine for it. Plans change. Expectations shift. The future we once pictured can transform into something entirely different. And yet, even in that uncertainty, life continues to unfold in ways we could never have predicted.*

*I would never have invited you here, Grief. No one does. But now that you are part of my story, I am learning to walk beside you rather than fight against you. You have reshaped the way I see the world, deepened my empathy, and reminded me to hold tightly to the moments of connection and love that make life meaningful.*

*So, while I may never fully welcome you, I acknowledge what you have taught me. And I carry those lessons forward as I continue to move through this life—one step at a time.*

*With honesty,*

*Me*

Grief is often spoken about as if it follows a clear path, moving steadily from pain toward acceptance. But grief rarely unfolds in a straight line. It circles back, sometimes years later, in moments that seem ordinary to everyone else but carry deep meaning for those who lived through the original experience.

For me, one of those moments came years after my son's suicide attempt, when many of his friends graduated from high school. It should have been a simple milestone, a celebration of young people stepping into the next stage of their lives. Instead, it quietly stirred something in me that I hadn't expected.

My son had chosen a different path. After everything we had been through, school no longer felt like the right environment for him, and he moved into the workforce instead. It was the right decision for him, and I respected that. I was proud that he had found a way forward that suited his wellbeing. But watching his friends celebrate their graduation still touched a tender place inside me.

In that moment, grief revisited.

Not grief for my son himself; he was here, living his life in his own way, but grief for the version of the story I once imagined. The simple narrative many parents carry quietly in their hearts: school, graduation, photographs with proud smiles, the shared sense of having reached a milestone together.

Seeing those celebrations reminded me that our family's path had changed. Our journey had taken turns we never expected, shaped by experiences that had altered the direction of things. And while I felt gratitude that my son was alive and finding his own way in the world, there was also a quiet ache for the path that had once seemed so certain.

This is something people do not often speak about: how grief can return long after the crisis has passed. It appears in milestones, in anniversaries, in moments when the world seems to be moving along a familiar script while your own story has taken a different route.

Over time, I have come to understand that this does not mean we are moving backwards. It simply means that grief is layered. It rises and settles again as life continues. Sometimes it asks us to acknowledge what has been lost, even while we celebrate what has been found.

And perhaps part of healing is learning to hold both gratitude and grief in the same moment, without needing to choose between them.

## CHAPTER FOUR
# THE DAYS AFTER

The sun rose that morning and arrived quietly, almost deceptively ordinary. The sunlight poured through the windows as if nothing had happened, yet the world felt irrevocably changed. Every sound, every shadow in the house reminded me that life as I knew it had shifted.

As the daily routine for my husband and younger son remained unchanged, I could not face work just yet, so I stayed home with my son. Somehow, the house felt emptier than ever, and I felt like the weight of responsibility rested entirely on me. Every decision, every precaution, every moment of attention was on me for the day. I was the sole anchor keeping my son tethered to safety.

On a practical level, I started searching the house for anything that needed to be removed or hidden away. I found myself looking at everyday objects through a new lens—not with panic, but with awareness. Things that had once blended into the background now asked for more careful consideration. The paramedics had removed all the strewn medication and did not give me back any of the remaining items. I cleaned out the medication cupboard at home and locked everything out of reach.

I started jotting down points to remember, things I noticed, or questions I wanted to follow up on each day. At this stage, I was truly trying to *'Stop the Blur'* (we will talk a bit more about this concept by Heidi Swapp later in the book).

While I wanted to curl up this morning and stay in bed, I knew this would not be helpful. We both showered, got dressed, and went out for a quiet lunch at a nearby café. When I went out during the day, I felt so broken inside. I imagined that people could see my failure, could read it in my expression, could somehow know what a terrible mother I had been. Each glance from a stranger, each nod from a passerby, felt like a judgment, confirming the harshest thoughts I carried about myself.

The hospital had advised that the outreach mental health team would call the next day. I waited, checking the phone repeatedly, listening for the ring, any sign that help was coming. But that call never happened. I reached out to them myself and booked an appointment for the 31st of October (11 days later, given we were due to fly out for a family holiday the following week).

It was a slow Friday nonetheless, with all of us watching a movie at home together that night. My son called in unavailable for work and shared what had happened with a friend who worked with him at the pizza store.

The first night after the attempt was the hardest. I lay awake in bed, long after my son had drifted into sleep. The doctors had mentioned that due to the tablets he had ingested, he may be more docile for the next few days.

Every creak of the floorboards, every sigh, every shift of the sheets made my heart race. I could not relax, could not allow myself to sleep deeply, knowing he was there, fragile and vulnerable, and that the responsibility of keeping him safe rested, I felt, entirely on me.

Exhaustion tugged at my body, but my mind refused to rest. I replayed the events of the previous day repeatedly, trying to understand, trying to pinpoint what I might have missed, what I could have done differently. Guilt wrapped itself around me like a heavy cloak. If only I had noticed something sooner. If only I had been more present. If only, if only…

When I reflect now on notes in my journal, the following days across the weekend, we tried to maintain a regular household routine of cleaning, mowing the lawns and gardening. Pizza for a Saturday night treat. We celebrated my younger son's birthday on Sunday, and I remembered wondering that if anyone knew of the past few days, how might they hug my son a bit tighter, or sit and cry with me, how they would thank God that it was not their experience. The shame inside me grew and grew.

The birthday party arrived with a mix of relief and dread. Outside, the sun shone, the garden was bright with balloons and decorations, and the smell of baking filled the air. Everything looked normal, even picturesque, but beneath the surface, my world was anything but.

Guests arrived, friends and family chatting happily, children laughing and running through the yard. My son interacted with everyone as usual, smiling, joking, and participating in games. No one suspected a thing. Was that the problem? He was good at masking his feelings, not showing others how he was really coping, or not, with life.

I must have also put on a good show, as no one asked how I was doing or what was wrong. My fear, my exhaustion and my grief were all carefully tucked away, hidden behind the mask of a parent hosting a birthday party. And yet, inside, I felt the weight of every unsaid word, every unseen tear, every quiet panic.

Yet there were moments, fleeting and fragile, where my son smiled, where he joined in a game, where he laughed softly. Each one of these moments became a beacon. I clung to them, desperate reminders that he was still here, capable of connection and of joy. Those glimpses were a quiet reassurance that we were still moving forward, even if it was only in small increments. The challenge was immense—how to maintain a sense of normalcy and celebration while carrying the heavy, silent knowledge of what could have been. Despite days passing, this consumed almost my every thought. It was after the event that I thought I might never be put back together.

As the party continued, I moved between hosting duties and careful observation, balancing my attention between both sons. I offered smiles, words of encouragement, laughter even, but inside, my heart was tense and watchful. Every clink of cutlery, every burst of laughter, every shout of delight reminded me that life goes on even in the shadow of trauma—but it also reminded me of the fragility of it all.

***Dear Me,***

*I see you tying balloons with shaking hands.*

*I see you checking the oven timer while your mind replays hospital corridors, safety plans, and midnight conversations no mother ever imagines having.*

*You are smiling for guests.*

*You are slicing cake.*

*You are saying, "Is everyone okay?"*

*And no one is asking if you are.*

*Today you are hosting a birthday party while your heart is still bruised.*

*You are wiping tables with one hand and steadying your breath with the other.*

*You are singing "Happy Birthday" while silently counting the hours since the crisis.*

*You are holding conversations about school and weather and decorations while carrying something much heavier beneath your ribs.*

*And yet — look at you.*

*You showed up.*

*You created normalcy in the middle of chaos.*

*You built a soft place for joy to land, even when you felt anything but joyful.*

*You protected the moment.*

*That is not pretending.*

*That is love.*

*It is okay that you feel split in two —*

*the mother who is breaking*

*and the mother who is baking.*

*Both are real.*

*Both are you.*

*No one sees the cost of what you are doing today.*

*They see balloons.*

*They see cake.*

*They see a capable woman.*

*But I see the courage it takes to keep the world steady for your children when your own world has tilted.*

*Later, when the guests leave and the house is quiet, you will exhale.*

*You might cry.*

*You might feel the exhaustion crash in.*

*That does not undo today.*

*Today you proved something important:*

*You can be devastated and devoted at the same time.*

*You can be fragile and functional.*

*You can be heartbroken and still create joy.*

*Be gentle with yourself tonight.*

*You are not "holding it together."*

*You are holding your family together.*

*And that is extraordinary.*

*With so much compassion,*

*Me*

By the end of the day, as guests departed and the house was quieter, I felt both exhaustion and a strange sense of accomplishment. The party had happened. We had celebrated. And yet, beneath it all, the vigilance remained, the weight of fear unrelieved. I knew that the days ahead would be long, that the work of healing would be quiet and persistent.

My son was working two casual jobs at this stage, so he managed to attend work on Sunday night and went off to school on Monday morning. In a low mood, I picked him up at lunchtime and shared some leftover birthday cake. He went off to his personal training session.

On Tuesday morning, the lowest of lows hit. I had read that after an incomplete suicide attempt, there may be a point where the person feels worse, guilty about what happened, and perhaps guilty that it was not complete. I called the mental health team, and they were able to see him that afternoon.

This was a busy day; we also met with the school to discuss class options and educational support, then met with our local doctor. He was very kind and considerate and appeared to listen actively to my son, again allowing me to attend the appointment.

Here in Australia, a General Practitioner (GP) is often the first professional person to see when you begin to experience symptoms of depression. Because GPs are trained to look at both physical and mental health, they play an important role in recognising when someone may be struggling emotionally and guiding them toward the right support.

When diagnosing depression, a GP usually begins with a conversation about how the person has been feeling. They may ask questions about mood, sleep, appetite, energy levels, concentration, and whether the person has lost interest in activities they normally enjoy. These questions help the doctor understand how long the symptoms have been present and how much they are affecting daily life. Depression is typically considered when low mood or loss of interest has persisted for at least two weeks or longer, alongside other emotional or physical symptoms.

GPs often use screening questionnaires to support the conversation. One of the most common is the Patient Health Questionnaire (PHQ-9), a short set of questions that helps assess the severity of depressive symptoms. These tools do not replace a clinical assessment, but they provide a structured way to understand what someone is experiencing.

Another important step is ruling out physical health issues that can mimic depression. A GP may ask about medical history, medications, and lifestyle factors, or order blood tests to check for conditions such as thyroid problems, vitamin deficiencies, or other factors that can affect mood.

Once a GP has gathered enough information, they will talk through possible next steps for support. This may include creating a Mental Health Treatment Plan (in Australia), which allows the person to access Medicare-subsidised sessions with a psychologist or other mental health professional. Depending on the situation, the GP may also discuss lifestyle strategies, therapy options, or medication.

For many people, this first appointment can feel daunting. Speaking about emotional pain is rarely easy. But a GP's role is not to judge or rush the process — it is to listen, assess, and help connect people with the care they need so they do not have to navigate their mental health challenges alone.

Our GP proceeded to diagnose my son with anxiety and depression and recommended antidepressant medication. For me, a diagnosis was not surprising, but somehow the process seemed like a tick-the-box exercise, nevertheless. Questions flooded my mind: *How did they get to know him in a brief 15-minute appointment? Why did this happen, and how can they prevent it from occurring again?*

Sitting in the GP's office during those early appointments felt strangely surreal. While the doctor asked careful questions and worked through the assessment process, my mind was racing far ahead of the moment. I listened to words like symptoms, screening, and treatment plans, trying to absorb what they meant for my child and for our family.

Part of me was grateful that there was a process, that someone knew the questions to ask and the steps to follow. But another part of me felt the quiet weight of it all with the realisation that we had crossed into a world I had never expected to enter as a parent. In those moments, I learned that seeking help often begins not with certainty, but with courage: the courage to sit in the room, to answer honestly, and to trust that even small steps toward understanding can lead toward healing.

In Australia, a landmark inquiry, the Royal Commission into Victoria's Mental Health System, was established to examine the deep and systemic problems in the delivery of mental health care. Over two years, it listened to thousands of voices—people with lived experience, families, carers, clinicians, and service providers—and revealed a system that was fragmented, under-resourced, and often focused on crisis and medication rather than ongoing, community-based support.

It found that trauma and the perspectives of carers were routinely overlooked, leaving families to navigate an overwhelming and complex system largely on their own. The Commission's 65 recommendations call for a system built around people's lives and needs, emphasising early intervention, integrated care, peer support, and the inclusion of families and carers in planning and treatment. Above all, it advocates a human rights approach that reduces stigma and ensures equitable access for all.

Reading these findings felt, in many ways, like they were telling my story. The gaps, the delays, and the lack of consistent support all mirrored my experience caring for my son. It was a reminder that these challenges are not personal failings, but part of a system that has long needed reform. At the same time, knowing that thousands of voices had been heard and that concrete change was being recommended gave me a mixture of relief and hope. Relief that our struggles were validated, and hope that future families navigating mental illness might find a system that listens, responds, and supports them before crisis takes hold.

***Dear Australian Mental Health System,***

*I am writing because I need to speak honestly about what I and so many others have experienced in your care. There is no denying that mental health services in our country exist to help people in crisis, but the reality is that the system is often slow, fragmented, and under-resourced. For those of us struggling, these delays are not minor inconveniences—they are gaps through which lives can slip.*

*Too often, people in urgent need of support face long wait times, confusing processes, or multiple disconnected points of contact. Families and individuals reach out for help, sometimes repeatedly, and yet the response does not arrive quickly enough. In that silence, suffering grows. People fall through the gaps, sometimes tragically, simply because no one advocates for them or helps them navigate the system.*

*Advocacy should not be optional—it should be embedded in the way care is provided. Many of us do not have the energy, knowledge, or resources to fight for the help we need when we are at our most vulnerable. Without timely intervention and compassionate guidance, mental illness can intensify, and hope can feel impossible to hold onto.*

*This letter is not intended to diminish the dedication of the professionals who work tirelessly within the system, but to highlight a structural reality: without quicker response times, better coordination, and built-in advocacy for those most at risk, the system fails to protect the people it is meant to serve. Real change is urgently needed so that no one is left waiting, unheard, or invisible.*

*People deserve to be seen. They deserve to be supported. They deserve a mental health system that acts with speed, care, and human understanding.*

*Sincerely,*

*Me*

I am pleased to say that my son has maintained a good working relationship with this local GP, who regularly reviews his medication and is supporting him holistically with his medical needs. The GP spoke to us about having the prescriptions dispensed and filled for me to ensure safe management and oversight. Thankfully, my son agreed with this.

A referral to a psychologist ensued, and we found an online service where my son could be seen within a few days. Again, gratefully, he allowed me to be present in the early sessions – I hope this helped him feel grounded and supported. I really felt blessed that I was 'the person' for my son. The one he could reach out to share his thoughts, sadness and frustration with.

With some strong advocacy on my part and phone calls when my son was at an all-time low, he was able to get an urgent appointment at the local mental health service – this was an eye-opener. Thankfully, my son was happy for me to sit in on the appointment until I was asked to wait in the waiting room while they spoke with him alone. The appointment went on for a long, long time – turns out they were writing a Safety Plan together. I sat in the waiting room, reading the brochures provided to me. Reviewing all the information on the noticeboards…over and over again.

***Dear My Son,***

*Today, they wrote a plan to keep you safe.*

*It sat there on the hospital desk — clinical words, structured steps, phone numbers, warning signs. Boxes ticked. Strategies listed. Names of people to call if the thoughts returned.*

*On paper, it looked manageable.*

*But what it really was… was hope in bullet points.*

*They asked you what your warning signs were.*

*They asked what helps.*

*They asked who you trust.*

*And you answered.*

*That mattered more than you realise.*

*Because a safety plan is not just about preventing harm.*

*It is about choosing to stay.*

*I watched you engage — tired, quiet, still fragile — but present. And in that small, fluorescent-lit cubicle, I saw something I hadn't seen earlier that day.*

*A thread.*

*Not certainty.*

*Not relief.*

*But a thread.*

*Something that said maybe you weren't entirely ready to let go.*

*I folded that plan carefully when we left. As if it were something sacred. As if those printed pages could hold the weight of my fear.*

*I know a piece of paper cannot fix what feels unbearable.*

*But it is a start.*

*And tonight, that is enough.*

*We don't need forever.*

*We just need the next hour.*

*The next day.*

*The next choice to stay.*

*And I will walk every single one of them with you.*

*Always,*

*Mum*

# CHAPTER FIVE
# THE DAYS FOLLOWING THOSE DAYS

## The Holiday

Before all of this had happened, we had a family holiday planned in Queensland. We didn't holiday often, and this was a big trip to celebrate my younger son's birthday.

It was meant to be a time of relaxation, a chance for my sons to play on the beach, for all of us to step away from the routines and pressures of daily life. But now, in the wake of this mental health crisis, the question of whether to go or not felt impossible.

I wrestled with conflicting thoughts. Part of me wanted to keep the plans as I clung to the idea of normalcy, hoping that a change of scenery might bring some relief, a sense of escape from the heaviness that I felt had settled over our lives. But another part of me was gripped by fear: *what if something happened while we were away? What if I could not monitor my son closely enough? What if the distance from home, from the support I could provide, became too dangerous?*

Every option felt weighted with risk and guilt. Choosing to stay home felt like giving in to fear, yet leaving for the holiday felt like abandoning my responsibility. I went over every detail in my mind: travel times, hotel arrangements, safety precautions, but the calculations brought no comfort.

In the end, the decision was not easy for me, and I knew that whatever choice we made, it would be scrutinised by my own anxiety, my relentless sense of responsibility, and the isolation that had become my constant companion. The holiday, for me, once a symbol of joy, now loomed as another test of vigilance, courage, and resilience.

As the holiday approached, anxiety plagued me. The thought of leaving home, even for a brief escape, felt unbearable. Every plan, every suitcase and all my preparation carried an undercurrent of fear. *Could I keep my son safe while away from the familiarity of home? Would the new environment trigger something I could not control?* The worry was constant, gnawing at me, leaving me restless and exhausted.

I remember telling my son afterwards that I wasn't sure if we should go on holiday. His response was simple and steady: "Why wouldn't we? I wouldn't let my brother down like that. That wouldn't be fair to him." In that moment, it hit me how effortlessly he could move forward, carrying empathy without fear, while I was still caught in a loop of my own thoughts, cycling through doubt, worry, and what-ifs. It was a quiet lesson in resilience; that even in the aftermath of trauma, life could continue, and that sometimes the courage to move forward doesn't come from grand gestures, but from a small, steady sense of responsibility and care for others. Watching him, I began to understand that my role wasn't just to protect or fix, but to hold space, to witness, and to trust in the strength he already carried.

We loved the Gold Coast, and Movie World is always a hit; the boys were ecstatic. The rides, the shows, the bright colours and loud sounds—all captivated them completely. For a few hours, I could see them simply being children again, laughing, shouting, and holding onto the thrill of each ride. Watching them, I felt a bittersweet mixture of joy and unease.

I wanted to show my sons, in some small, metaphorical way, that I could be brave too. So, I joined them on a roller coaster. I hate heights. I also hate roller coasters, yet they thought it was the funniest thing ever. I truly thought that if I could get through how I had been feeling, I could certainly ride The Green Lantern! Perhaps I was wrong with the metaphor, but I held on tight and closed my eyes the whole ride.

Even amidst the excitement of the holiday, the shadow of the previous week never fully lifted for me and I didn't sleep well. I remained hyper-aware of my older son, scanning for signs of distress, moments of withdrawal, or sudden irritability. The restlessness that had begun before the trip persisted, manifesting as short bursts of frustration or tension, seemingly without a clear cause. He could sense the unease within himself but could not fully articulate it, and I tried to provide both reassurance and gentle boundaries without smothering him.

One night, the restlessness arrived at the dinner table while eating out at a restaurant for my younger son's birthday. My older son could not identify why he was feeling this way -perhaps the medications he was trialling (strangely enough, they warn that the antidepressant medication can increase suicidal ideation!); we were not sure. I was desperately trying to think of ways to burn off this feeling, so, funnily enough, we ended up in an unusual, almost desperate family activity: the gym.

We moved together, lifting, stretching, walking on the treadmill—anything to distract and redirect some of that restless energy. It was not a normal birthday night, and yet, in a strange way, it became a moment of connection – anyone who knows me knows that a gym is not a place I would usually be found! My husband and younger son joined us, and the physical activity allowed tension to release, gave a temporary reprieve from the weight of fear, and reminded us, in small ways, that we were still a family capable of shared experiences. It came to an end when we were kicked out of the gym for having an underage child in there, even though we were being cautious and had the place to ourselves.

Each day was a careful balance between allowing him to enjoy the activities: the rides, the shows, the endless novelty of a new environment, while monitoring for the subtle cues that something might be wrong. I was constantly alert, walking the fine line between participation and vigilance.

***Dear My Son,***

*Today was loud.*

*Rollercoasters rattled overhead. Music spilled from speakers. Children ran past with fairy floss and sunburnt noses. You laughed — properly laughed — head back, eyes bright, arguing about which ride was the best and insisting we go again.*

*And for hours, you were just a teenager at a theme park.*

*Not a patient.*

*Not a risk assessment.*

*Not a safety plan folded in my handbag.*

*Just you.*

*I watched you in the queue lines. I watched your shoulders loosen. I watched you check your phone less. I watched colour return to your face in a way that made something inside me unclench — just a little.*

*But here is the truth I won't say out loud:*

*Even on the rollercoaster, I was counting.*

*Counting your mood shifts.*

*Counting how long since the hospital.*

*Counting signs.*

*Counting breaths.*

*Joy now comes with a shadow. Not because I don't trust you, but because I am learning how fragile relief can feel.*

*When you ran ahead to the next ride, my heart still skipped.*

*When you went quiet for a moment, I noticed.*

*When you smiled, I memorised it.*

*I hate that fear sits beside happiness now.*

*I hate that I cannot simply relax into the day the way I used to.*

*But I also see something important.*

*You showed up today.*

*You participated.*

*You teased your brother.*

*You complained about the lines.*

*You rolled your eyes at me.*

*You lived.*

*And maybe that is what healing looks like at first, not grand declarations or dramatic breakthroughs, but ordinary days stitched carefully back together.*

*I am still worried. I probably will be for a while.*

*But today gave me something steady to hold onto.*

*Your laugh on the drop.*

*Your grin in the pictures with Batman and Bugs Bunny.*

*Your voice saying, "That was actually so good."*

*If worry is the price of loving you this fiercely, I will pay it.*

*But today, my beautiful boy, you gave me more than fear.*

*You gave me hope that joy is still possible.*

*And that matters more than you know.*

*Always,*

*Mum*

I remember my son had wandered off when we were on holiday at the Wet 'n' Wild water park. I became highly anxious, looked all over the park for him, tried calling his phone, and tracked him on the Life 360 app. I could not find him anywhere. My thoughts went to the darkest of places – *what if something terrible happened on this holiday? How would I ever be able to reconcile this decision to come? What about the impact on others...* my mind was going crazy. Turns out, just before I went to enter the men's amenities, he came walking out. He had some difficulties with the plumbing in there and was delayed in returning to us. Oh, my heart!

In the quiet moments, when the boys were occupied or asleep, I returned to my journalling. I had started capturing my daily thoughts, literally trying to *'Stop the Blur'* of each day. Each day, I jotted down 3-4 things I wanted to remember or was grateful for. Some days, that was all I could manage.

The pages of my journal became my container, a sanctuary where I could release the whirlwind of fear, guilt, and anxiety that lingered even during moments of outward normalcy. Writing gave voice to the emotions I could not speak aloud, helped me process the tension that came with my son's restlessness, and reminded me that survival was about more than physical safety. It was about sustaining emotional endurance, for both him and me. At the time, I didn't understand mental ill health, and I couldn't make sense of why it had appeared so suddenly and so viciously at our doorstep.

On the days when I could manage more than a few points, the act of writing was meditative. It gave me a place just to focus on myself for a short while. I documented the small victories: a smile shared, a ride enjoyed, a brief conversation that hinted at the return of normalcy. I also wrote about the fears that lurked beneath every interaction, the exhaustion that weighed on me even in moments of apparent calm, and the realisation that I had to be both protector and witness, constantly present in a state of quiet vigilance.

By the end of the holiday, I understood something crucial. Despite the anxiety, the restlessness, and the constant undercurrent of fear, moments of connection and joy were still possible. I had learned that bravery took many forms; sometimes it was screaming on a roller coaster or monitoring my child while he slept. At other times, it was simply putting pen to paper to confront the chaos within.

The holiday became a lesson in endurance, observation, and the quiet strength required to face each day. And it was in those small, painstaking acts of showing up, holding space, writing it down, that I began to reclaim a sense of control, a fragile yet undeniable foothold in a world that had been upended. Who knew this was the holiday we needed to take together after all?

Next was the return to school for my son and work for me, but the days were far from predictable. Often, my son could not make it the whole day at school. We had established an emote icon of a purple umbrella as a signal he wasn't coping so well. The Mental Health team suggested the use of a symbol, so he didn't need to explain to me each time how he was feeling and what he needed from me. The 'purple umbrella' text message indicated that he felt unsafe and he needed to come home. The signal became both a lifeline and a source of tension.

On one hand, it allowed him to communicate without words, giving him some control over his environment. On the other hand, it filled me with anxiety, a constant uncertainty about when it might appear, and what that day would look like once it did.

Every morning, as I prepared him for school, I carried the weight of anticipation. *Would today be the day he could stay all day? Or would the signal come, summoning me to collect him early? How am I supposed to work and plan to be away from home just in case?* Even when he arrived home safely, my mind raced, cataloguing the signs I might have missed, wondering if the restlessness, the tension, or the subtle cues of distress had been overlooked.

Yet there was a strange reassurance in these moments. At least if he was home, I could see him, monitor him, and intervene if needed. I could provide a sense of stability, structure, and reassurance that was impossible to guarantee elsewhere. While the uncertainty of school days was a source of constant anxiety, it also reinforced the centrality of my role in his care. I was both observer and anchor, fully present, entirely responsible, and utterly alone in that vigilance.

Side note- Years later now, I have, funnily and subsequently, developed an aversion to a text message alert sound, and I almost always keep my phone on silent.

**Journal entry from November 2023**

*Eating hurts my stomach, and I am rarely tasting the food – I am just eating because I'd better eat something. Thoughts are of continual doubt and fear. I cannot work and deal with the matters happening there at the moment. I cannot stop replaying what happened, the words said and the aftermath. I am scared for the future, each day, and what it will bring.*

*I am cancelling my planned trip to Adelaide and will lose money for everything paid, but it doesn't matter. I do not have a reliable support system to hold me up or care for my family if I am away. I have not told my mother – I don't want to worry her. I have no one.*

*My child is going to die one day, and I don't know what else to do to prevent this.*

As the weeks passed, it became clear that the unpredictability of school days could not continue indefinitely. My anxiety over whether he would make it through a full day, combined with the toll it was taking on him, prompted a conversation with the school. We spoke openly about what he needed to complete the year and what accommodations could be made. I must say the school were wonderful and open to providing support in any way they could.

After careful discussion, it was agreed that my son could finish up a bit earlier than the usual end of term. This adjustment provided a small but meaningful relief. It acknowledged his limits, his ongoing recovery, and the need to balance educational requirements with emotional wellbeing. The decision did not feel like giving up; rather, it felt like a practical, compassionate step, and the recognition that his safety and mental health came first.

I quickly realised, and still feel this way to this very day, that I can relax more when my boys are home. The relief of having a clear plan, a more predictable endpoint for the school year, gave both of us a little breathing room. For the first time since the crisis, there was a framework to the day that allowed me to shift from constant panic to measured observation.

However, as a family, we made some small, intentional changes to our routines. On weekends, we went for family walks. The outings were brief and, honestly, attempts to get us all out of the house. They became a symbol of a concerted effort to spend more meaningful time together. Every step, every conversation along the path, or shared laugh was a reminder that life could still hold connection and joy, even in the shadow of fear.

The hardest part I found in talking to anyone was trying to find the words to explain what had happened, to give a 'reason' that others could understand, and to help them follow the journey with us. With a visible injury, like a broken leg, it's easy because people see the damage, and the path to recovery feels clear. Mental ill health is different. It isn't something that can be fixed with the right food, more exercise, or simple solutions. And because it is invisible, I carried a heavy weight of blame and guilt for the impact it had on our family, especially in response to comments and assumptions from others. That silence and misunderstanding made the struggle feel even more isolating.

*"We are taught that suicidal ideas are extreme...abnormal, ill, selfish, taboo, uncomfortable, uncommon...toxic, indulgent...insane and wrong. This seems like a lot of baggage to place on what seems like a lot of baggage.*

*Perhaps the idea is that judgment will act like a deterrent...If we pretend suicidal thoughts are rare, then suicide itself will become rare.*

*If we say suicide five times in a mirror, will it suddenly appear like Candyman? Or will we just make a profoundly isolating experience feel even lonelier?"*

**Campbell Walker**

As a mother, negative comments or minimising remarks about my son's mental health didn't just affect him; they landed on me too. As his mother, hearing people suggest that "He just needs to eat better" or "He should exercise more" felt like a dismissal of everything I was doing to keep him safe and supported. It undermined my confidence in my judgment, intuition, and ability to hold him through a crisis. Every time someone reduced his struggles to something simple, it added weight to my shoulders with a silent question: *Am I doing enough? Am I missing something?* It amplified the loneliness, the pressure, and the constant hyper-vigilance I already carried.

It's more than just hurt feelings. Comments like these can chip away at the quiet strength parents rely on in moments of fear and uncertainty. They make you question yourself, even when you are doing everything in your power to protect and love your child.

Acknowledging this doesn't mean placing blame entirely on others, but it does capture the emotional landscape of motherhood in a crisis: the fatigue, the vulnerability, and the constant need to stand firm when the world doesn't always understand the weight of what's happening behind your closed doors.

***Dear You,***

*I know you mean well.*

*When you say, "Maybe he just needs to eat better."*

*When you suggest more sleep, more sunshine, and more exercise.*

*When you talk about routine, discipline, and resilience.*

*I know you are reaching for something practical. Something fixable. Something that makes the world feel less frightening.*

*But I need you to understand something gently and clearly.*

*Mental health struggles are not a salad deficiency.*

*They are not a skipped gym session.*

*They are not laziness.*

*They are not a lack of gratitude.*

*When someone is in the depths of depression or crisis, their brain is not simply "sad." It is overwhelmed. Dysregulated. Flooded. Sometimes frighteningly dark. Logic does not cut through it the way you imagine it would.*

*Yes — food matters.*

*Yes — movement helps.*

*Yes — sunlight and routine are supportive.*

*But they are supports, not cures.*

*Telling someone in crisis to "just exercise" can feel like telling someone with a broken leg to go for a run. The advice may be technically healthy, but it misses the injury.*

*What helps more than solutions is presence.*

*Instead of:*

*"Have you tried eating better?"*

*Try:*

*"I don't fully understand this, but I want to."*

*Instead of:*

*"You just need to push through."*

*Try:*

*"That sounds heavy. How can I support you?"*

*Mental health recovery is complex. It can involve therapy, medication, safety planning, professional support, time, patience, and sometimes simply surviving one day at a time.*

*What people in crisis need most is not optimisation.*

*They need compassion.*

*You don't have to become an expert.*

*You don't have to fix it.*

*You just have to resist the urge to reduce it.*

*Because when you minimise something this serious, even unintentionally, it can make someone feel unseen — or worse, ashamed.*

*And shame is fuel for silence.*

*I know it's uncomfortable to sit with something you can't fix.*

*It's uncomfortable for us too.*

*But if you want to help, sit with us anyway.*

*Listen. Learn. Ask. Stay.*

*That is more powerful than any diet plan.*

*With honesty and hope,*

*Me*

**Reaching out**

Reaching out to share my experience was harder than I ever imagined. It felt like admitting a weakness I wasn't allowed to have, like exposing a part of myself I was supposed to be able to control. When I finally found the courage to speak up, the response was not what I had hoped for. There was hesitation, misunderstanding, and at times, a quiet dismissal of what I was feeling. The very act of asking for support, something so human and necessary, became a reminder of how isolating it can be to carry mental health struggles alone.

I remember the day when I shared this unfolding crisis with one other person, a friend who had invited me out for a coffee. As we sat opposite each other at a local café, she asked how I was, and that was it. I lost it. Crying in public is not something I wanted to do, but I had held this in for so long. Overwhelmingly, someone had asked ME how I was doing! It felt like a question I had been waiting so long for, and I became overcome with emotion.

The difficult part is that she never really followed up after that. We might say hello or exchange a few words, but there was no message or check-in afterwards. I felt shame so intensely at this time. I felt like I had re-entered the local community, feeling vulnerable, and I had failed to keep my family intact. I felt like I was the only one this had happened to and had shown my broken heart in public.

The response I received and the way I felt surprised me at the time and still now as I reflect on the impact of this event. However, I have come to realise that mental health, even now, is something many people don't know how to talk about or feel unsure about discussing. I had made the shame my own, but I was not alone. Despite feeling deeply embarrassed about it, I now know I am not alone.

Looking back, I can see that my own response may have been too intense. I was carrying so much emotion that it was hard to contain in that moment, so perhaps a busy coffee shop wasn't the best place for me to share such intense emotions.

If you want to share your own challenges with a friend, I can now offer some advice on how to do so. There are gentle ways to do it that won't feel overwhelming for either of you. A message, a quiet check-in, or simply expressing that you need someone to listen can create space for connection without pressure.

You could start by asking if you can talk about something that has been worrying you.

*"My son has been struggling with some mental health challenges lately. It's been scary at times, and I've been feeling a lot of fear and guilt as a parent. I don't expect you to have all the answers; I just needed someone to listen."*

You don't have to share everything at once. Choose what feels safe to talk about and give yourself permission to pause or redirect if you feel overwhelmed. Sometimes friends want to help but don't know how. Saying something like, *"I just need you to listen right now" or "I'm not looking for advice, I just need someone to be here"* helps them understand how to support you.

Not every friend will respond in the same way. Some people are naturally empathetic; others may struggle to hear what you're saying. It's okay to share with those you feel safest with first. Mental health is a part of life. Remind yourself, and your friends, that sharing struggles doesn't make you weak; it makes you human. If you're talking about your child's mental health, focus on the experience rather than labels: *"My son has been struggling lately, and I'm worried about him"* rather than overly clinical terms that can feel alienating or frightening.

You can end the conversation by thanking your friend.

*"Thank you for listening. It really helps just to say it out loud and know I'm not carrying it all on my own. I've also been keeping a journal to work through my thoughts; it's been a lifeline for me."*

You don't have to carry the burden silently as I did, but you also don't have to over-explain. Your feelings and your story are valid, just as they are. It's okay if a conversation doesn't go perfectly. This can be difficult and can make you feel worse after the chat. Remember, though, that talking about mental health is messy and emotional; that's normal. What matters is that you reach out rather than isolate yourself. This is a hard lesson I learned along the way.

Talking about mental ill health in your own home can be surprisingly difficult, even though you might expect it to feel safe. A mental illness is not one person's fault, and remember, it's not like a broken leg, where you have a defined timeframe for healing. It can go on and on and come and go. Then it seems dormant and pops up repeatedly without warning.

My experience was that even with people we love, there was a fear of being misunderstood, judged, or seen as 'overreacting.' I was worried that family members would minimise my feelings or blame themselves, or me, if I spoke openly.

Home is where emotions often feel most intense. Seeing your child struggle or even reliving your own mental health challenges or those of past family members in that environment can make conversations feel too heavy or overwhelming. Sometimes, it feels safer to postpone the discussion rather than risk conflict or distress.

Families often have developed unspoken rules about what is 'okay to talk about.' Mental health may be one of those topics that have been historically avoided, creating a pattern of silence. I understand it can be difficult to grasp and breaking that pattern can feel risky.

At home, it's not always easy to speak about what's going on in your head or heart. There's a weight that comes with the fear of upsetting someone, of being misunderstood, or of breaking the rhythm of daily life. As a mother, I often felt the need to be strong, to keep my children safe from worry, even while my own thoughts were heavy and tangled.

Journalling became my quiet refuge. A place to untangle the knots, to name the fears I couldn't voice aloud, and to give my heart a safe space to speak. On the page, I could feel everything, the worry, the guilt, the exhaustion, without worrying about how it might land on someone else. It was here, in these private words, that I could honour my own feelings and start to understand the 'mama heart' that carries so much, often in silence.

On the upside, though, over time, it felt as though my son and I were becoming closer. In the aftermath of the crisis, I became my son's go-to, trustworthy person who he relied on when the rest of the world felt overwhelming or unpredictable.

I was able to gain insight into my son's inner world in ways I might never have imagined. I began to understand his fears, sensitivities, and triggers. Mental health challenges often open the door to more honest, vulnerable dialogue. We have been able to share thoughts, feelings, and fears we wouldn't have discussed otherwise, creating a deeper emotional connection.

By showing up consistently, listening without judgment, and respecting his pace, I hope my son has learnt that he can rely on me. That trust can become the foundation for long-term security and resilience. I've also become more aware of my own limits and the importance of self-care. Watching him navigate his emotions has taught me strategies to stay calm, to regulate my own fears, and to remain present even when everything feels uncertain. It's a strange, humbling kind of mutual learning: we both teach and support each other, sometimes without words.

Even in the midst of these small successes, journalling remained essential.

**Journal entry from 27th November 2023**

*My son refused to go to school due to anxiety. I am at a total loss as to how to help. I try talking to him, rationalise the feelings and he gets angry, won't talk and shuts down. I can't make him go to school I feel sick all the time and don't want to be here. My younger son had a meltdown and I cop it all! It's all on me…then trying to work through it all feels impossible.*

My own mental health began to spiral, and I felt profoundly alone, as though there was no one I could reach out to. I remember writing in my journal on 29 November 2023 about the physical toll it was taking, with terrible stomach pain, and a quiet, overwhelming wish to simply fall asleep and not wake, to escape the weight of it all.

I don't share these words lightly. But I have come to understand that these kinds of thoughts, as confronting as they are, can surface for many carers. They are felt more often than they are spoken, carried silently in the spaces where exhaustion, fear, and helplessness meet.

After a young person has attempted suicide, it's not uncommon for parents or carers to experience intrusive thoughts, including suicidal ideation. The emotional impact can be intense: fear, helplessness, exhaustion, grief, and the constant state of alert can overwhelm your nervous system. Sometimes the mind goes to dark places, not because you want to act on those thoughts, but because you're trying to cope with something deeply distressing.

That said, while it can be a human and understandable response, it's also something that deserves care and support for you. You don't have to carry that alone.

A few important things to keep in mind:

- These thoughts don't define you or mean you want to harm yourself—they often reflect overwhelm and emotional overload.
- Carers can experience secondary trauma or burnout, especially in mental health crises.
- Getting support is not only okay—it's essential.

If you're comfortable, it might help to:

- Talk to a trusted person (friend, family member, counsellor)
- Connect with a GP or mental health professional
- Reach out to carer-specific supports (there are services just for people in your position)

If you're in Australia, you can also reach out to:

- Lifeline (13 11 14) – 24/7 support
- Suicide Call Back Service (1300 659 467) – counselling for people affected by suicide
- Carer Gateway (1800 422 737) – support specifically for carers

If these thoughts are becoming stronger, more frequent, or feel like something you might act on, it's very important to seek immediate help, either by calling one of the above or going to the nearest emergency department.

You've been carrying something incredibly heavy. It makes sense that it's affecting you. You deserve support, safety, and space to be cared for, too.

*"Could it be true that one has to experience in order to understand? I have always denied this idea, and yet of motherhood, for me at least, it seems to be the case".*

**Rachel Cusk**

We often hear the cliché that you would do anything for your child, but in those moments, it no longer felt like a cliché; it felt real. I would have given up anything, everything, if it meant my son could be free from pain and self-loathing. I just wanted him to see what I could see: his beauty, his worth, and the incredible potential he carries within him.

**Myths to Bust**

I think it is important here to include some of the myths about mental ill health that I have heard or that have been asked of me throughout my experience.

There are many myths about mental health that continue to shape how people understand and respond to it. One common myth is that mental illness is simply a sign of weakness or that people could 'snap out of it' if they tried hard enough. Conditions such as depression, anxiety disorders, or bipolar disorder are complex health conditions influenced by biological, psychological, and social factors. Suggesting that someone should simply be stronger or more positive ignores the very real challenges people face and can make individuals feel blamed for something beyond their control.

Another myth is that people with mental ill health are unpredictable or dangerous. This belief has been reinforced by media portrayals and misunderstanding, but it does not reflect reality. Most people experiencing mental health difficulties are far more likely to withdraw or struggle quietly than to harm others. In fact, they are often more vulnerable to discrimination, isolation, and misunderstanding because of these stereotypes.

A further misconception is that mental health problems are rare or happen only to certain kinds of people. The one that popped into my mind was – how can successful professionals have a child with mental illness? How naïve I was, because the truth is that mental health challenges can affect anyone, regardless of age, background, profession, or personality. Many people live with mental health conditions while continuing to work, parent, study, and contribute meaningfully to their communities. Because so many individuals mask their struggles, mental illness often remains invisible to those around them.

There is also a persistent myth that talking about suicide will 'put the idea into someone's head.' Research has shown the opposite to be true. Open, compassionate conversations can create space for people to share what they are feeling and seek support. Avoiding the topic out of fear can leave individuals feeling even more isolated in their distress.

Finally, some people believe that recovery from mental illness is impossible, or that once someone experiences a mental health condition, it will define them forever. While some conditions may require long-term management, many people recover or learn ways to live fulfilling lives alongside their mental health challenges. With understanding, support, and appropriate care, hope and healing are very real possibilities.

I also wanted to mention medication use here, as opinions about medication for mental illness can vary widely, even among professionals, families, and people who have lived experience. For some, medication represents an essential part of treatment, a tool that can stabilise mood, reduce overwhelming symptoms, and make it possible to engage in therapy or everyday life. Medications such as antidepressants, mood stabilisers, or antipsychotics are often prescribed for conditions like depression, bipolar disorder, or schizophrenia, and many people describe them as life changing. They can provide relief from symptoms that once felt unmanageable, offering a sense of steadiness that had previously been out of reach.

At the same time, others hold more cautious views about psychiatric medication. Some people worry about side effects, the process of finding the right medication, or the feeling of becoming dependent on something to regulate their emotions or thinking. It is not uncommon for individuals to go through a period of trial and adjustment before finding a medication that works well for them, and that process can sometimes be frustrating or discouraging. Because of this, some people prefer to focus first on psychological therapies, lifestyle changes, or supportive interventions before considering medication.

There are also broader philosophical differences in how people think about treating mental health conditions. Some view medication as a necessary medical response to biological illness, while others see mental distress as something deeply connected to life experiences, trauma, or social circumstances that cannot be solved by medication alone. In practice, many clinicians encourage a balanced approach, where medication is considered one part of a larger picture that may also include therapy, social support, and personal coping strategies.

Within families and communities, these differing opinions can sometimes create tension. One person may strongly believe medication is necessary, while another may fear it will dull personality or take away a sense of control or that the young person can simply improve their health with diet and exercise. Navigating these perspectives can be challenging, particularly when someone is already vulnerable. Ultimately, decisions about medication are uniquely personal and often evolve over time as individuals work with healthcare professionals to find the approach that best supports their wellbeing.

**The next diagnosis**

My son began to engage with a psychologist through online appointments, and he permitted me to sit in with him on several of the sessions. Our sessions with the psychologist were an eye-opening journey. Firstly, observing him sit still for an hour, listen to the questions, and watch my son respond honestly—or sometimes hesitantly—gave me insight into his inner world in a way I had never experienced before.

It was suggested after some time that my son may consider assessment for ADHD, given his presentation and conversations throughout those sessions. We were luckily able to get in to see a local paediatrician (of whom my younger son is a patient) and proceeded to work through the criteria for this diagnosis. It wasn't just a checklist; it was a detailed exploration of his behaviour, attention, and thought patterns over time.

In case you are interested, the comprehensive assessment included a clinical interview to discuss personal and developmental history, behavioural observations, and medical and family history. We completed questionnaires and rating scales and sought input from teachers, my son, and me as the parent.

We reviewed school reports, daily routines, emotional responses, and even sleep patterns. What initially felt like a maze became a map, helping us understand why some things were harder for him, why certain situations triggered overwhelm, and why he experienced life differently from his peers. I felt like we were finally putting together the pieces of a puzzle I didn't know I could solve.

The ADHD diagnosis is then made according to DSM-5 criteria (Diagnostic and Statistical Manual of Mental Disorders). The criteria for diagnosis must include:

- Persistent inattention and/or hyperactivity-impulsivity
- Symptoms present before age 12
- Symptoms occur in multiple settings (school, home, work)
- Clear evidence of functional impairment

A deep sense of guilt sat with me throughout this process. My mind kept returning to the same questions: *How did I not recognise this earlier? How was it never identified or even raised as a possibility?*

At every parent-teacher interview over the years, we were told a familiar story—he was talkative, sometimes disruptive, but capable of doing well if he would just focus. Those words shaped how I understood him at the time. And yet, looking back now, things seem clearer, almost as though the pieces were there all along, just not arranged in a way that made sense.

For a while, I told myself I had failed him. If I am honest, I still think this and can become fixated on it.

But over time, I have come to see this more gently. I worked with the information I had, just as the teachers and professionals did. None of us had the full picture. None of us could see what we didn't yet understand.

The 'what ifs' still surfaced: *What if this had been recognised earlier? Could things have been different? Could we have avoided the mental health crisis that followed?* These questions don't have answers, and I have had to learn to sit with that uncertainty.

There was also a quieter, more confronting reflection: *How could I be working in the disability field and not have seen this in my own home?* But even that, I have come to understand differently. Being close to someone you love can sometimes make it harder to see clearly. Love does not always come with objectivity; it comes with hope, with trust, and with the belief that things will unfold as they should.

What I know now is this: I did not fail him. I was there. I cared. I showed up repeatedly with the knowledge and understanding I had at the time. And when I learned more, I adapted, just as any parent would.

This journey has taught me that hindsight brings clarity, but it should also bring compassion, for us as much as for those we love.

Research shows that children, teens, and adults with ADHD are at a higher risk of suicidal thoughts and behaviours compared to those without ADHD. This doesn't mean every person with ADHD will experience this, but certain factors increase risk.

The elements that can occur with ADHD, and were certainly observable in my son, include the following:

Impulsivity (difficulty regulating impulses) can make moments of distress more dangerous, as decisions may be made without considering long-term consequences.

Emotional dysregulation (intense emotions, mood swings, and difficulty calming down) can increase feelings of hopelessness or overwhelm.

Co-occurring mental health conditions, such as anxiety, depression, or trauma, which often co-occur with ADHD, are significant risk factors for suicidal ideation.

Frustration and repeated setbacks: struggling academically or socially, feeling misunderstood, or experiencing repeated failure, can erode self-esteem and contribute to despair.

Without early recognition and strategies for coping, ADHD symptoms can intensify stress, hopelessness, and isolation. I was assured that early intervention, like counselling, skills coaching, and creating a personal safety plan, is key. Understanding these dynamics helped provide structure, empathy, and consistent support while remaining vigilant and responsive. Working alongside the psychologist and my son to develop some boundaries and mutual understanding was sometimes very helpful.

Seeking help was never about having all the answers. It was about opening a door, having my son involved and engaged in the process, being willing to face the unknown, and trusting someone to guide us through it. Through the psychologist and paediatrician's questions, observations, and explanations, I learned not just about ADHD, but about how to truly see my son and myself in the process.

One of the thoughts that stayed with me, quietly but persistently, was the fear of what a diagnosis might mean for my son. Not just in terms of support or understanding, but in how it might shape the way he saw himself—and how the world might see him.

I worried about the idea of a *'label.'*

*Would it define him in ways that felt limiting? Would people see the diagnosis before they saw him?* I found myself wondering how it might follow him into school, into friendships, into the future he was still trying to find his way toward.

And then there was a deeper concern about how he would carry it. *How would he make sense of it within himself?* I didn't want him to feel reduced to a diagnosis, or to believe that it somehow explained all of who he was. He had always been so much more than that; complex, capable, thoughtful in ways that didn't always fit neatly into expectations.

At the same time, I held another, quieter understanding. Without a name for what he was experiencing, there had been confusion, misunderstanding, frustration, and a sense that he was somehow getting it wrong. Teachers had described behaviours, but not always the reasons behind them. And I began to wonder if, rather than limiting him, a diagnosis might offer something else: clarity, language, and a way to better understand himself.

I found myself caught between these two thoughts: the fear of a label, and the possibility that it could bring relief.

Over time, my perspective began to shift. I started to see that a diagnosis does not have to define a person; it can simply describe one part of their experience. It can be a tool, not a limitation. Something that opens doors to support, understanding, and self-awareness, rather than closing them.

What mattered most was how it was held, both by him and those around him. Not as something that diminished him, but as something that helped explain the way he moved through the world.

I still carried that protective instinct, that desire to shield him from judgment or misunderstanding. But I also began to see that understanding himself fully and honestly might be one of the most empowering things he could be given.

What I hadn't expected was the way he would respond to it. Where I had held fear, he seemed to find clarity.

He didn't resist the diagnosis. He embraced it. The paediatrician spoke openly with him about the diagnosis and discussed options for medications, which really empowered him throughout the process.

Rather than seeing it as a label that would limit him, he began to use it to understand himself. It gave language to things he had struggled to explain—why certain environments felt overwhelming, why focus could come and go, why his mind seemed to move in ways that didn't always align with expectations.

It was as though something clicked into place for him.

Instead of asking, *"What's wrong with me"?* There was a shift toward *"This is how my brain works."* And in that shift, I saw a sense of relief I hadn't anticipated. The confusion that had once surrounded him softened. In its place came curiosity, even acceptance.

He began to recognise his patterns, to understand his strengths alongside his challenges. What I had feared might define him gave him a framework, a way to navigate the world with greater self-awareness.

Watching this unfold changed something in me, too.

I realised that the meaning of a diagnosis is not fixed; it is shaped by how it is understood and carried. Where I had seen the risk of limitation, he found an explanation. Where I had worried about stigma, he found a starting point for self-awareness.

In many ways, he led the way.

He showed me that this was not about placing him in a box but about giving him tools to understand how he experiences life. And through his acceptance, I began to let go of some of my own fears.

Because in the end, it was never about the label. It was about what it made possible: understanding, self-compassion, and a new way forward.

I learned early on that ADHD isn't just about restlessness or difficulty focusing, but that it can affect emotions, impulse control, and self-esteem in ways I hadn't fully understood. Research shows that children and teens with ADHD can be at higher risk of suicidal thoughts and behaviours, not because of who they are, but because of the intensity of their emotions, the frustration of repeated setbacks, and the way impulsivity can magnify moments of despair.

ADHD isn't always visible. A child may look like they're 'just being difficult,' or an adult may appear perfectly composed on the outside. But inside, there can be a constant undercurrent of shame, self-doubt, and frustration. For my son, I have no doubt this was the case. I have read that teens with ADHD know they aren't meeting expectations, whether at school, at work, or at home, but they don't fully understand why. They feel different, 'less than,' or somehow failing, even when their intentions are good. Over time, this can grow into chronic self-criticism, anxiety, or even depressive thoughts.

As mentioned previously, this had never been recognised at school – sure, he 'talked too much,' and was disruptive in class with his peers, but with the years of disrupted schooling throughout COVID, the restlessness and disengagement could have been easily explained. We know this is not a moral failing, but a byproduct of a brain that functions differently, combined with a world (school and at home) that expects conformity.

***Dear My Resilient Son,***

*I know this diagnosis may feel like a lot to take in all at once.*

*You might be feeling relief, confusion, or even frustration—and all of that is okay. ADHD doesn't define who you are. It doesn't mean you're "less than" or "broken." It simply means your brain works a little differently, and that comes with its own strengths and challenges.*

*There may be days when focus feels impossible, when emotions feel too big, or when it seems like the world expects you to fit a way that doesn't come naturally. I want you to know that none of that is your fault. You're not lazy, you're not failing, and you're not alone.*

*This diagnosis is a tool, not a limitation. It's a way to understand yourself better, to see patterns, and to find strategies that work for you. You get to learn what helps you thrive—what routines, supports, and self-care practices make life feel a little lighter. You also get to define your own pace and your own path.*

*Some days will be frustrating, some days exhausting, and that's normal. But there will also be victories—big and small—that remind you of your resilience, creativity, and determination. And when it feels overwhelming, it's okay to ask for help. You don't have to face this alone.*

*Most importantly, remember this: ADHD is only one part of who you are. It doesn't take away your worth, your brilliance, or your heart. Be kind to yourself, celebrate the small wins, and know that you have people who believe in you—even on the days when you can't believe in yourself.*

*With care and belief in you,*
*Me*

I believe our growing awareness and compassionate support of my son, along with his own understanding of why he now sees the world in a particular way, can help reduce the shame and replace it with understanding, self-acceptance, and hope.

When your child is struggling with ADHD, which may impact their mental wellbeing, people offer a lot of advice. Some of it is helpful, some of it isn't, and some of it simply doesn't fit your child or your family. Over time, I realised that what helped the most were not grand solutions or perfect systems. It was the small, steady things that built trust and safety between us.

The first thing that truly helped was learning to listen differently. Instead of trying to fix every problem or jump in with solutions, I started by simply sitting with him and listening to what he was saying. Sometimes he didn't want advice. Sometimes he just needed someone to acknowledge that what he was feeling was real and difficult.

Another important step was bringing in professional support. Accessing a paediatrician and psychologist helped both of us understand ADHD in a way we hadn't before. It gave us language for things that had previously just felt confusing or overwhelming. It also reminded me that I didn't have to carry everything alone. Having someone guide us through strategies and coping skills made the journey feel less isolating.

Structure also made a difference. ADHD brains often thrive on routine, even when they resist it at first. Gentle routines around sleep, schoolwork, and daily tasks created a sense of stability. We learned to break things down into smaller steps and celebrate progress rather than perfection.

One of the most important lessons for me was to focus on his strengths. ADHD can make a young person feel like they are constantly falling short of expectations. But when I started to actively point out his creativity, his humour, his kindness, and his resilience, I could see his confidence slowly rebuilding.

Perhaps most importantly, I learned that presence matters more than perfection. There were many days when I worried that I was saying the wrong thing or not doing enough. But simply being there and showing up, checking in, and reminding him that he was loved no matter what, became the strongest support I could offer.

This journey hasn't been simple, and it certainly hasn't been perfect. But through patience, support, and a willingness to keep learning, we found ways to move forward together.

Helping someone with ADHD and mental illness is not about fixing them. It's about creating an environment where they feel understood, supported, and capable of growing.

Where my story begins - with Mum

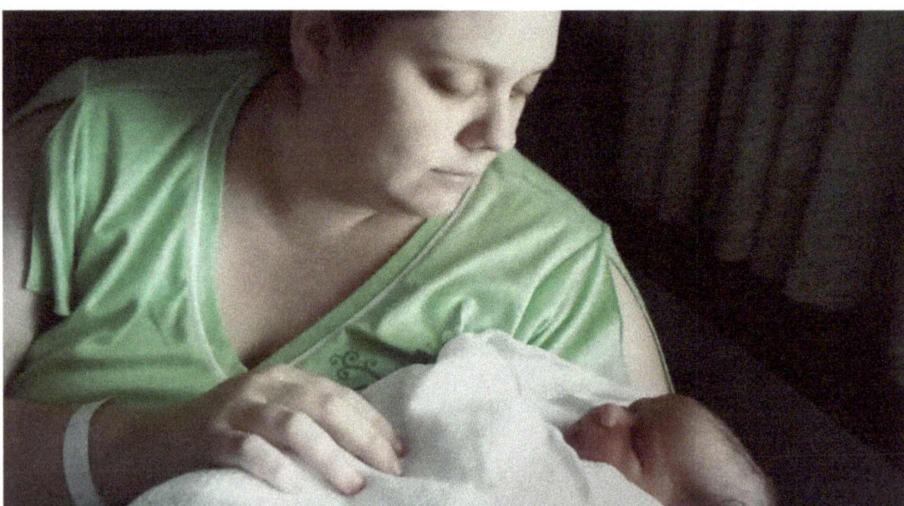

The day I finally became a mum

Early days of parenting - I still can't believe I get to be your mum

Celebrating my son's first birthday

Remembering our baby boy

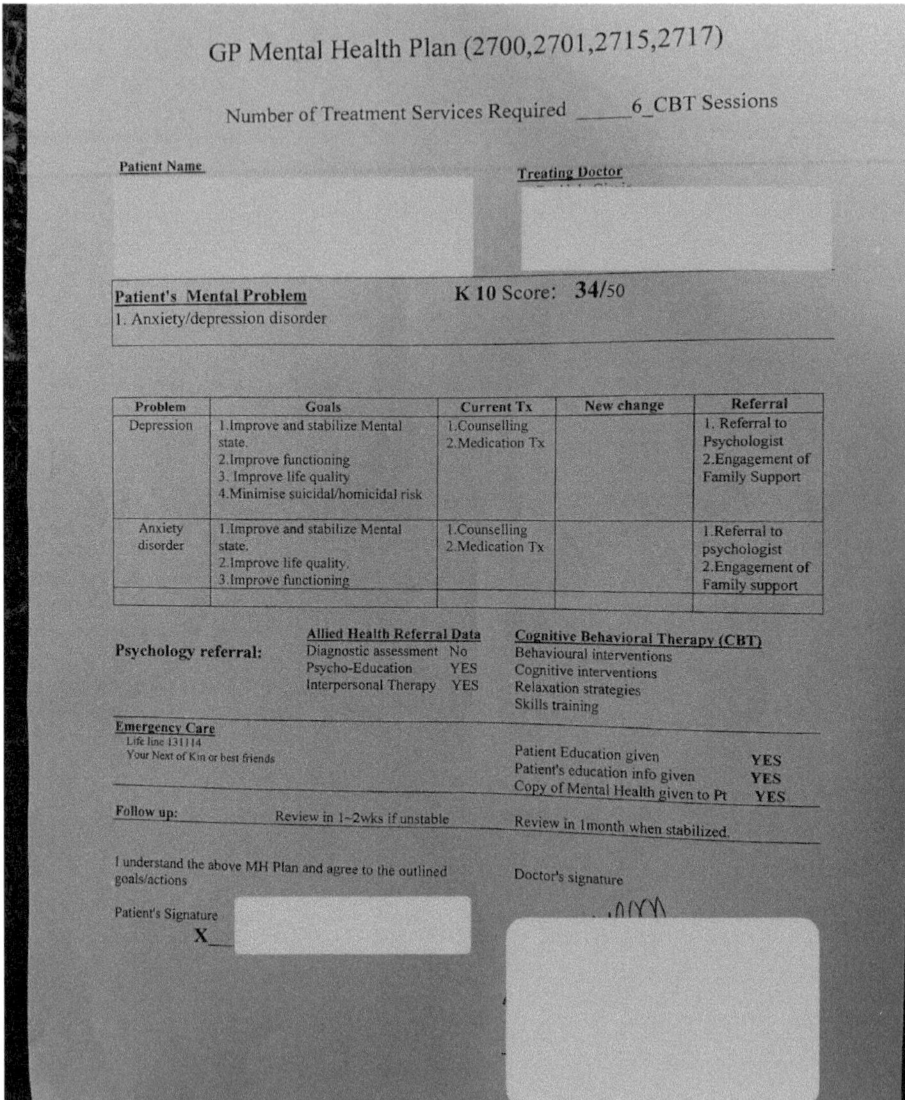

GP Mental Health Plan (2700,2701,2715,2717)

Number of Treatment Services Required ______6_CBT Sessions

**Patient Name** | **Treating Doctor**

**Patient's Mental Problem** | **K 10 Score: 34/50**

1. Anxiety/depression disorder

| Problem | Goals | Current Tx | New change | Referral |
|---|---|---|---|---|
| Depression | 1.Improve and stabilize Mental state.<br>2.Improve functioning<br>3. Improve life quality<br>4.Minimise suicidal/homicidal risk | 1.Counselling<br>2.Medication Tx | | 1. Referral to Psychologist<br>2.Engagement of Family Support |
| Anxiety disorder | 1.Improve and stabilize Mental state.<br>2.Improve life quality.<br>3.Improve functioning | 1.Counselling<br>2.Medication Tx | | 1.Referral to psychologist<br>2.Engagement of Family support |
| | | | | |

**Psychology referral:**

**Allied Health Referral Data**
Diagnostic assessment No
Psycho-Education YES
Interpersonal Therapy YES

**Cognitive Behavioral Therapy (CBT)**
Behavioural interventions
Cognitive interventions
Relaxation strategies
Skills training

**Emergency Care**
Life line 131114
Your Next of Kin or best friends

Patient Education given YES
Patient's education info given YES
Copy of Mental Health given to Pt YES

**Follow up:** Review in 1~2wks if unstable Review in 1month when stabilized.

I understand the above MH Plan and agree to the outlined goals/actions

Doctor's signature

Patient's Signature

X__

Initial GP Mental Health Plan

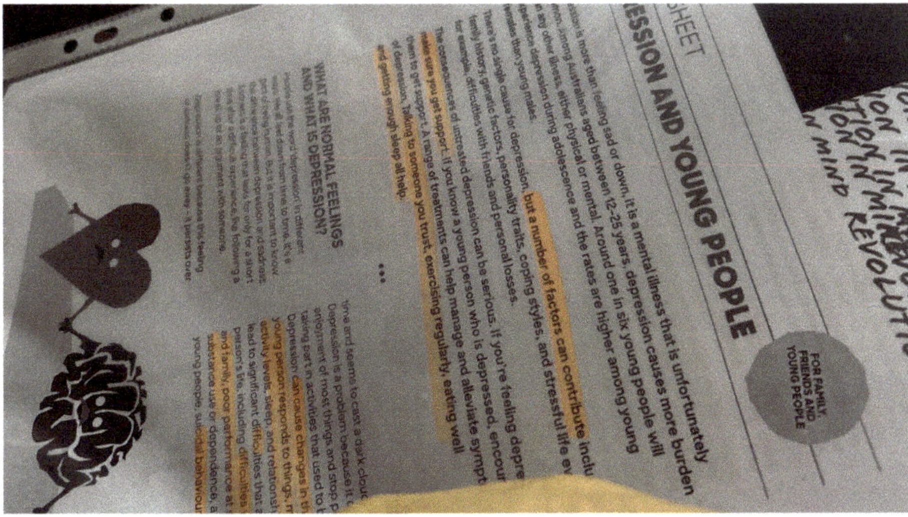


Knowledge matters - learning about depression so we can support each other

Some pages hold more than just words

Smiles and fun times on a family holiday - October 2023

Just them and the view at Mt Cannibal

Family, love and a little Christmas sparkle

Journalling for me now is about intentional writing as a tool for self-awareness and personal growth.

Journal coaching helps you slow down long enough to notice the stories you've been living within.

Looking forward to supporting the formation of online Journalling Circles

CHAPTER SIX

# THE FORGOTTEN FAMILY MEMBERS

When a young person experiences a mental health crisis or attempts suicide, the immediate focus understandably turns to the person in danger. Doctors, psychologists, hospitals, and support services mobilise around them, trying to stabilise the situation and create a pathway toward recovery. This care is essential. But within that necessary focus, something quieter often happens inside the family: the experiences of siblings and other family members can fade into the background.

It is important to mention siblings here. They may be described as the 'forgotten family members' in mental health crises. They can be deeply affected by a sibling's mental illness or suicide attempt, often carrying worry, fear, and confusion that they struggle to express. Many siblings in the research report feeling anxious about their sibling's safety, uncertain about what is happening, and unsure whether they are allowed to talk about it openly. Yet despite this emotional impact, there are relatively few services designed specifically to support siblings through these experiences.

In many families, siblings quietly adjust to the new reality without being asked how they are coping. They may notice the sudden change in atmosphere at home, the whispered conversations, the hospital visits, and the way attention shifts almost entirely toward the young person in crisis.

Some siblings respond by becoming more independent, trying not to add to their parents' worries. Others carry fear they do not know how to voice. Research has shown that younger siblings, in particular, can experience significant emotional strain when a brother or sister has attempted suicide or is experiencing severe mental health challenges.

There is also a complex emotional balance that siblings must navigate. They may feel love and concern for their brother or sister while also feeling frightened, frustrated, or even resentful of the disruption to family life.

These feelings can be confusing, especially for young people who may not yet have the language to understand them. Without safe spaces to talk openly, siblings sometimes carry these emotions alone.

Families themselves often receive limited guidance on how to support siblings during this time. Parents are understandably consumed with managing risk, coordinating care, and trying to hold the family together. Yet siblings may also need reassurance, information, and opportunities to express their own experiences. Studies exploring sibling experiences following suicide or severe mental illness highlight how important it is for siblings to feel heard and included, rather than invisible within the family system.

Over time, however, many siblings also develop remarkable empathy and emotional awareness through these experiences. Living through a sibling's suicide attempt can open a young person's heart in ways that everyday life rarely demands. Witnessing the pain, fear, and vulnerability of someone they love forces them to step outside themselves and truly consider another person's inner world. They learn to listen beyond words, to read emotions in subtle gestures, and to sense distress before it is spoken.

They see firsthand the impact of isolation, shame, and fear, which teaches them compassion grounded in lived experience rather than theory. This kind of empathy is often quiet and understated — a sensitivity to others' struggles that grows naturally from having loved someone through one of life's most terrifying moments. It can shape them into someone profoundly aware, patient, and compassionate, with an understanding of human fragility and resilience that is rare at any age.

When families create space for open conversations, reflection, or creative outlets such as writing, art, or journalling, siblings can begin to process what they have witnessed and felt. Just as journalling became a place of reflection and healing for me, it can also offer siblings a quiet space to understand their own emotions and make sense of difficult moments.

Mental health crises do not happen to one person alone; they ripple through the entire family. Recognising the experiences of siblings is not about taking attention away from the child in crisis. Rather, it is about acknowledging that healing is a family process and that every family member deserves understanding, compassion, and support along the way.

The service system, and rightly so, is focused on the patient at the time of the suicide attempt occurring. Survivors of suicide attempts may feel relief that their loved one is alive, but that relief often comes tangled with continued anxiety, anger, or confusion. The paradox of 'thankful but scared' can be emotionally exhausting.

There is often an intense fear that it could happen again. Parents, siblings, and loved ones may find themselves constantly alert, checking in, and struggling to relax. The nervous system can remain in 'high alert' mode for days, sometimes weeks, leaving people physically and mentally exhausted.

At the local Mental Health service, I recall being handed a fact sheet on *Depression and Young People* to read while waiting for my son at his appointment. I do not recall any direct conversations with any service providers about flyers for sibling or family support, and the opportunity to discuss our thoughts after a suicide attempt.

I have often heard from others that even though the person is alive, there is mourning for the innocence, safety, and normalcy that were disrupted. I certainly could resonate with this. Families often grieve the changes in their relationships, routines, and sense of security, and the intensity of these feelings can lead to emotional numbness, disconnection, or difficulty processing daily life. This was certainly the case for me. This was, I think, my nervous system's protective response, giving me space to survive the immediate aftermath.

On the flip side, amid the fear and grief, relationships may deepen. Families can experience profound moments of empathy, tenderness, and connection, recognising life's fragility and resilience.

I only noticed recently that the GP Mental Health Treatment Plan for my son mentioned Engagement of Family Support. I assume this means support for the family, but it did not come.

I have since found some resources that families can access to support them through this time – a free online support for family and friends of someone who has attempted suicide (see resources at the end of this book), and local groups will often be open to customising their post-suicide programs to support family members when needed.

The next days passed in a blur of monitoring, quiet conversations, and constant observation. I stayed close, didn't sleep much, hoping that my presence alone could anchor him, even if nothing else could.

Throughout this time, I noticed significant changes within my younger son, also including an increase in behavioural outbursts and significant anxiety around sleep. He would often sleep on a mattress on the floor of his brother's bedroom. Again, looking back on my daily journalling helps me remember this as I am writing, coming up to three years later.

When a teenager faces a mental health crisis, as we touched upon previously, the spotlight naturally falls on them, understandably so. But the siblings, the brothers and sisters living in the same home, experience the ripples of that event too. They feel fear, confusion, guilt, and even anger, often silently, because they don't want to add to the family's already present stress. Their love is just as real, yet it can go unseen, unspoken, and unacknowledged.

One of the ways siblings can navigate this emotional landscape is through journalling or creative expression. Writing, drawing, or other reflective activities give them a safe place to process feelings they may not yet know how to voice. It allows them to name their fears, express frustration, and explore hope without the pressure to explain or justify their emotions to anyone else. Through these outlets, they can reflect on what is happening, understand their own responses, and even gain a sense of agency in a situation that often feels completely out of their control.

Encouraging siblings to engage in reflection doesn't replace the support they need from parents or professionals, but it can give them a private space to process, to breathe, and to feel heard, even in solitude. Just as journalling became a lifeline for me, it can become a quiet companion for siblings, helping them navigate the uncertainty and intensity of a family mental health crisis. It reminds them that their experiences matter, that their emotions are valid, and that they, too, are part of the journey toward healing.

With more perspective, I now wish I had handled this better and provided my younger son with ways to understand and express his feelings more effectively. Creative outlets can help them feel seen, heard, and supported — even privately. Here are some ideas:

**1. Journalling Prompts:**

- "Today I felt... because..."
- "One thing I wish people understood about me is..."
- "A moment today that gave me hope was..."
- "If I could speak to my sibling without anyone listening, I would say..."

**2. Expressive Arts:**

- Drawing or painting emotions: using colours, shapes, or symbols to show feelings that are hard to put into words.
- Collage or scrapbooking: creating visual stories of daily life, positive memories, or hopes for the future.

**3. Reflection Letters:**

- Writing a letter to themselves about their day, their feelings, or their hopes.
- Writing a letter to their sibling in crisis (even if they don't send it) as a way to express love, support, or questions.

**4. Guided Check-ins:**

- Setting aside 5–10 minutes each day to write or draw, helping them process what they are feeling in a consistent, low-pressure way.
- Pairing reflection with a calming ritual — a favourite song, tea, or a walk — to make the process feel safe and grounded.

**5. Sharing (if comfortable):**

- Encouraging siblings to share their reflections with a parent, trusted adult, or counsellor if they feel ready.
- Emphasising that it's okay to keep some things private — reflection is as much about understanding oneself as it is about communicating with others.

Through these exercises, siblings can find a sense of control, a safe space for their emotions, and a way to acknowledge the difficult and confusing experiences they witness. Journalling and creative reflection can help them navigate feelings of fear, guilt, frustration, or love, just as it did for parents, and remind them that their experiences matter too.

***Dear Younger Son,***

*I can't imagine how heavy everything must feel right now. Seeing your brother struggle, knowing he tried to end his life—it shakes something deep inside all of us. I wish I could take away the fear, the confusion, the guilt that keeps creeping in, but I can't. All I can do is sit beside you, holding space for your feelings, and remind you that you are not alone in this.*

*It's okay to feel angry, scared, or even numb. It's okay to cry, or to shut the world out for a little while. None of this means you are weak—it means you are human, and you are caring deeply for someone you love. What happened is not your fault. We cannot control someone else's choices and trying to carry that weight only makes it heavier.*

*If you can, try to let yourself lean on others—family, friends, or someone trained to help. Talking about what you are feeling doesn't make it any easier for him, but it can make it bearable for you. We must take care of ourselves, too, even when it feels impossible.*

*I don't have the right words to fix this. There is no simple way to make it okay. But I want you to know that I am here, that we are in this together, and that hope can still exist, even in the shadow of what we just lived through. You are not alone. And neither is he.*

*With love,*
*Mum*

## CHAPTER SEVEN
# STOPPING THE BLUR

Through all of this—the fear, the uncertainty, the new strategies, the professional appointments, and the small victories—I realised that information and understanding alone weren't enough. Knowing the risks, the strategies, and the steps to take didn't ease the weight on my heart. What I needed was a way to process it all, to name my fears, capture the moments of joy and terror, and make sense of the constant swirl of thoughts.

That's where journalling became essential. It wasn't just a record of events; it became a container for everything I carried: the raw emotions, the unanswered questions, the relief, the hope. Writing allowed me to slow down, witness the story as it unfolded, and stay grounded even when the world around me felt unsteady.

So, what is journalling exactly? Yes, it is words on a page or on a digital platform, but it really opens a door to greater self-awareness. Throughout the process, if you are willing, you learn more about who you are and what you want for your life.

By taking the time to reflect on yourself, your experiences on a regular basis, journalling invites you to get to know yourself. How deep you go with it depends on you. I have always been a naturally curious person and have enjoyed writing, though it certainly has been a process for me to develop my use of writing for wellness.

Benefits for me have included self-discovery, stress reduction and greater awareness and learning. Hence, the title of this book: *So Who Are You Anyway?* When your whole world shifts and you begin to question everything you ever knew, the person you thought you were, the roles you play in your family and community life, this question seemed relevant.

It started because everything felt like a blur. It is what I have always done, but different this time.

Hospital lights.
Forms.
Conversations I half-remembered.
Words and phrases like 'risk assessment' and 'safety plan.'
The way time both crawled and disappeared.

I started writing because I was terrified the fear, the panic and the endless 'what ifs' would all dissolve into a single, indistinguishable blur. I needed to hold it still, to slow it down enough that I could see it, name it, and somehow survive it. Even though revisiting the details was painful, I knew I would need them someday, not just to remember, but to make sense of what had happened.

Writing became the only place I could breathe, where the chaos could take shape on the page, and I could face it without being consumed. So, I wrote.

At first, it wasn't brave or literary. It was messy. Fragmented. Notes in the margins of my day, often a short note on the app of my phone. Half sentences. Questions I didn't know how to answer. Things I was too afraid to say out loud.

But something shifted.

When I wrote it down, the fear stopped circling quite so fast.
When I named it, it felt less monstrous. It was particularly useful when I had no one to talk to.
When I described the hospital cubicle, the fluorescent light, the sound of my son's crying — it became a memory I could hold instead of a storm I was trapped inside.

Writing didn't fix anything.

It didn't make the risk disappear or make the nights easier. Though it did share the weight.

The page became a place where I didn't have to be composed or be the steady mother. I didn't have to reassure anyone.

On the page, I could admit:

*"I am terrified."*
*"I don't know what I'm doing."*
*"I am holding it together by threads."*

And somehow, saying that, even privately, steadied me.

Because blur is overwhelming.

But words create edges.

And edges are something you can hold.

Journalling began almost out of necessity. In the first days after my son's crisis point, the world felt too heavy, too fractured to navigate without some form of anchor. The thoughts, the fear and the guilt all crowded in, unrelenting, impossible to share with anyone. As others around me continued their usual daily routine, the outreach call never came, and family and friends remained unaware. I was alone. Writing became the only way to hold myself together.

A renowned paper crafter, designer and entrepreneur, Heidi Swapp is a huge inspiration to me. I had followed her professional career for many, many years, but her personal experience was a particular beacon of light for me throughout this time.

Following the tragic loss of her son Cory to suicide in 2015, Heidi has been an advocate for suicide prevention, and I'd like to explore this a little here and share what was most helpful to me. Whilst our experiences are different, I often think about the support and strength Heidi has shared with others in her journey of loss and grief, and how important it has been—when I may not feel comfortable talking about this with others—to have someone I could reach out to and take some solace from.

It is the concept of Heidi Swapp's *'Stop the Blur'* that I have subscribed to for many years now. *'Stop the Blur'* encourages you to jot down 3-4 details and snippets each day, that act as a record that become doorways to your memories and stories of every day. I have done and continue to do this daily; however, it became even more integral during the crisis.

Heidi says, "Our lives are moving faster than ever before, and our brains can easily become overloaded. That doesn't mean that we don't have the memories stored, we do! It just means that it's trickier to access our memories, making it possible to forget." I will include the link to Heidi's website at the end of this book, but my journal became a container for my thoughts. A way for me to get through each day and capture the basic thoughts, points of gratitude, etc., in one place – my journal.

'Don't freak out' is a key phrase and philosophy used by Heidi Swapp. I recall regularly repeating this to myself again and even sharing it with my husband at times, encouraging a sense of calm in myself to build trust with my son and foster connection. This was particularly important in the context of supporting his mental health (and also my own).

Key aspects of this message focus on preventative parenting – for me, this means I am in control of how I respond. As Heidi says, "Managing one's own reactions to 'messes, accidents and grades' is key to creating a safe space for open communication and preventing the escalation of emotional crises".

At one point, I even considered getting a 'Don't Freak Out' tattoo on my arm just to remind me to manage my own reactions and to create an open, supportive relationship with my son. Heidi's words on one of her Instagram posts resonate deeply with me. She said, "The process of grieving Cory's loss and continual contemplating of what could have possibly prevented the outcome of his death is daily consciousness for me."

Heidi goes on to say something like this - "Having a child who has completed suicide is an absolutely devastating circumstance AND has been a giant catalyst for change. I believe with my whole heart that CONNECTION is the best suicide prevention…this is what I believe is the greatest change we can strive to make DAILY to improve our relationships and create that essential connection. Here it is: DON'T FREAK OUT, and moms, it starts with us!"

You can see why I find Heidi and her story inspiring, and they kept me going during this time. Paired with love, passion, and a mom heart for storytelling, memory-keeping, and strong mental health advocacy, it brought me light during dark times.

Largely, Heidi's advice is to 'dial down' the panic, focus on regulating our own emotions and incidentally, this helps to build stronger relationships and trust. I was grateful to remember these points on the nights I would sit on the bedroom floor next to my son's bed. When he would share with me his thoughts about not wanting to be here and not knowing why he felt this way. I would repeat it in my head: *Stay calm, don't freak out… tell him we are here to support him.*

A core component of this message, says Heidi Swapp, is to 'forgive yourself'. Ultimately, it encourages parents to forgive themselves for not knowing what they didn't know. I continue to work on this one, even now.

***Dear Heidi,***

*I want to thank you.*

*Your courage in speaking openly about mental health and suicide prevention has quietly reached so many people — including me. Your advocacy reminds me that hope and fear can exist side by side, and that sharing our stories can truly make a difference.*

*Reading about your journey has been a lifeline. It has reminded me that even in the scariest moments, awareness, intention, and love matter. You've inspired me to write more intentionally and to notice, reflect, and give words to both the struggles and the small victories.*

*Knowing someone else has walked this path and used their voice to help others has made me feel less alone. Your work has not only shown me the power of sharing a story, but also the importance of showing up, even when the day feels impossible.*

*With respect and gratitude,*

*Me*

Now, let's get back to how journalling and jotting down these details helped me work through thoughts and next steps.

At first, the words were very practical and often noted in my phone notes app. I noted changes in moods, behaviours and any other observations. But very quickly, the pages became something more: a safe space where I could unburden myself. I could name the fear that had no voice, the guilt that no one acknowledged, the exhaustion that no one could see. I could write down the chaos without judgment, without interruption or expectation.

**Journal entry from 7 October 2024**

*Carers leave today. My son has a doctor's appointment this afternoon after disclosing thoughts of self-harm last night, thankfully not following through. Almost a year to the date. He is going to be contacted by the mental health team, and the GP has reviewed his medication dosage.*

Every day, I tried to write, even if only a few lines. Some days, the words came in a torrent, raw and jagged, spilling every thought and emotion I could not otherwise release. Other days, I wrote carefully, meticulously documenting the small signs of progress alongside any questions I wanted to explore or thoughts I had.

**Journal entry from 19 October 2024**

*One year since my son tried to take his life by overdose. It feels like yesterday, and it's been the worst year of my life. Worrying constantly, and I've never experienced anxiety like this before. Loneliness and isolation are extraordinary.*

But it was more than observation—it was survival. The act of putting pen to paper anchored me when the world felt unsteady. Each word was a small claim to control, a declaration that I was present, that I was watching, that I was holding both myself and my son with intention and care. The pages were silent companions, never questioning, never judging, simply holding the truth of what had happened and what was happening now.

Journalling quickly became more than just a record of events. It became somewhere to put the parts of the day that left me raw.

Writing it down slowed me enough to see patterns I might have missed in the rush of surviving. It gave me something steadier than my fear. Something I could look at and say and understand a little more, *"This is what's happening. This is what he needs"*.

Somewhere along the way, I realised I wasn't only writing about him. I was writing about myself.

At first, the notes were focused outward — his moods, his sleep, his words, the things professionals might ask about. I told myself it was for clarity. For appointments. For tracking progress.

But between the lines, I was leaving traces of myself:

The exhaustion.
The second-guessing.
The way I held my breath every time my phone buzzed during school hours.
The guilt when I felt frustrated.
The relief when I heard him laugh.

I hadn't meant to document my own unravelling. But it was there, threaded through every entry.

And slowly, the writing stopped being just surveillance.

It became a reflection.

I wasn't just asking, "How is he today?"
I was asking, *"How am I carrying this? How am I feeling today?"*
*"What does it mean to love someone through something you cannot fix?"*

The page became the one place I didn't have to be composed. I didn't have to reassure anyone. I didn't have to soften the truth.

I could admit that I was frightened. That I was tired. I sometimes felt alone in a room full of people. And the more honest I was, the more the writing shifted again.

It wasn't just coping anymore. It felt like witnessing. Witnessing my son's fight and my own. Witnessing the quiet, invisible work of holding a family together while everything feels uncertain.

And then one day, it occurred to me that maybe this wasn't only about surviving a season. Maybe it was about honouring it. Not in a dramatic way. Not in a 'look how strong we are' way. But in a truthful way. The messy middle. The contradictions. The love that sits right next to fear.

What began as a way to stop the blur had become something steadier. Because if I needed these words to make sense of it, maybe someone else would too. I didn't set out to write a book. I set out to survive a season.

But the pages kept growing. The notes became paragraphs. The paragraphs began to carry weight, and I wondered what others supporting a loved one through mental illness were experiencing. As we often heard stories of local teenagers in our local area taking their own lives, I wondered if my words, my son's insight, might be able to help other people.

It was a story. Not a polished one. Not a triumphant one. But a real one — full of fear and doubt and love and small, stubborn hope. It wasn't just about what happened to us.

It was about what it means to mother in the middle of uncertainty. To love someone fiercely while learning that you cannot control the outcome. To sit with darkness and still look for light.

Somewhere between the daily details and the quiet confessions, the writing stopped being private survival and started becoming something braver.

It became a way to say, "This happened. This is how it felt." And you are not alone if it feels this way for you, too. That was the moment I understood — I wasn't just stopping the blur anymore. I was shaping it. And just maybe, shaping it meant it could help carry someone else through theirs.

I began to see how much I had silenced myself in daily life, always pushing forward but not sharing with those closest to me, always prioritising others. Journalling gave me permission to put my own experience at the centre. I wrote about the isolation of keeping this secret, the shame and guilt I felt in not really telling anyone.

***Dear My Son,***

*We survived that night.*

*There were days after it when I wasn't sure how we would. When everything felt fragile — like glass under our feet.*

*I carried fear like a second skin for a long time. I watched you breathe at night. I listened for shifts in your mood. I measured silence.*

*But here's what I've learned:*

*You are not broken.*
*You were overwhelmed.*

*You are not weak.*
*You were exhausted from holding too much inside.*

*And I am not a failed mother.*
*I am a mother who stayed.*

*We are still teaching each other. Still rebuilding trust. Still figuring out what openness really looks like.*

*But you are here.*

*And that is everything.*

*Forever in your corner,*
*Mum*

## The Themes in My Journalling

As I spent more time journalling, I noticed patterns; recurring themes that revealed not just my thoughts, but the deeper currents shaping my life. Grief emerged repeatedly, sometimes quiet and lingering, sometimes raw and urgent. Anxiety and fear surfaced in waves, often linked to moments when I felt powerless or uncertain. But so did hope, curiosity, and glimpses of joy; tiny sparks that reminded me that not every moment was defined by struggle.

Other themes revealed themselves through reflection: resilience, the challenge of boundaries, the push and pull of love and responsibility, and the ongoing work of understanding myself as both a parent and a person. Journalling became a map of my internal world, showing where I was stuck, where I was growing, and where the lessons of my experiences were slowly taking root.

I also noticed that my journalling often returned to questions rather than answers: *How do I navigate this situation? What does it mean to be present? How can I hold both love and frustration without losing myself?* These questions didn't always need answers—they were signposts pointing me toward awareness and insight.

Over time, the act of writing became more than processing; it became exploration. Each page was a space to notice patterns, to test ideas, and to gently shift perspectives. Through journalling, I could track the evolution of my thoughts and feelings, see growth that wasn't always visible in the day-to-day, and begin to rewrite the narratives I had been carrying for years.

When I look back at my journals from those early days, I don't just see words on a page, but I see myself, raw and stripped down. The themes that emerged weren't tidy or organised at the time. They were messy, emotional, and often repetitive, looping like a song I couldn't get out of my head. Now I can see them clearly: guilt, isolation, anger, questions of identity, the craving for control, and, surprisingly, small glimpses of hope.

When I look back over those months of journalling, I can see the undercurrents more clearly than I could at the time.

Guilt was woven through almost every page.

It hid inside ordinary sentences. In the way I questioned my decisions. How I replayed conversations. I kept circling the same thoughts — what I should have noticed, what I might have missed, whether loving him fiercely should somehow have protected him from this.

### Journal entry from 8 February 2024

*I got myself worked up into a state this morning – my son was in a mood and refused to get ready, declaring he would shower and walk to school once we left. I hid the meds and played scenarios in my mind about what could happen, how I would react and even what I would say. Grateful we have agreed on the Life 360 app, and I could see him walking safely to school. All was fine, but it took me hours to calm down again, and I felt on edge all day.*

I was trying to take responsibility for something that was never mine to control, and my nervous system was in overdrive!

Alongside the guilt was a deep, quiet isolation. There were people around me. School pick-ups still happened. Groceries were bought. Birthday candles were lit. Life, on the surface, looked unchanged.

But inside our home and inside my head, everything had shifted. I carried knowledge others didn't hold. I knew how close we had come to losing him. I knew how fragile the days could be. That kind of knowing separates you. Even in a crowded room, you can feel alone with it.

### What I Wish I Had Asked My Husband

Looking back now, I sometimes wonder what might have been different if I had asked my husband more about how he was feeling during that time.

In the middle of a crisis, my focus was entirely on our son: making sure he was safe, finding support, trying to understand what had happened and what we needed to do next. My own emotions were overwhelming enough, and I often assumed that my husband was simply coping in his own way.

But with time and reflection, I have come to realise that parents can carry these experiences very differently. While I often needed to talk, write, and process my thoughts out loud, he sometimes held things more quietly. At the time, I didn't always know how to bridge that difference.

Now I sometimes think about the questions I wish I had asked.

*Are you okay?"*

*What has this been like for you?*

*What are you worried about most?*

*How can we support each other through this?*

Those questions were not absent because we didn't care about each other. They were absent because the situation itself felt so overwhelming. It felt like all my energy went into protecting our child, managing appointments, navigating school, and simply trying to get through each day.

What I have learned and reflected on since is that partners often share the same fears and love, even when they express them differently. Sometimes one person speaks while the other steadies the ground beneath the family. Both roles are important, even if they are not always understood in the moment.

If there is one thing I would say to parents walking a similar path, it is this: amidst caring for your child, try to make space for each other too. Even a small conversation can remind you that you are not facing the storm alone.

Because beneath the exhaustion, the worry, and the uncertainty, there is usually the same thing holding both parents steady: the quiet, determined love for their child and for the family they are trying to protect.

There were many thoughts and questions during that time that I didn't always say out loud. Some felt too heavy, others too uncertain, and some I simply didn't yet understand myself. It was often easier to sit quietly with my journal and let the words find their way onto the page. Writing became a place where I could explore what I was feeling without judgment or expectation.

It allowed me to acknowledge fears, frustrations, and small moments of hope that might otherwise have remained buried beneath the practical demands of each day. In many ways, the journal became the conversation I was not always able to have; a quiet space where the complexities of motherhood, marriage, and survival could coexist.

The journal became the one place that understood without explanation, no matter how brief the entries were.

**Journal entry from 25 March 2024**

*My son managed a full day at school today. A good day.*

And then there was anger. I felt ashamed to admit this, but I did desperately wish things could be different. I was angry at the unfairness of it all and at the detour our lives had taken, which is now part of our story. Angry at how quickly life can tilt and at how casually some people reduced something so serious to simple solutions. And I was angry at how this impacted me so deeply, and at the service systems that felt slow to respond when urgency lived in my chest.

Sometimes I was angry at the version of life we used to have, its naïve ease. The assumption that tomorrow would look like today. Writing let me admit that anger without judging it. It let me say, " This is hard. This is not what I expected. This hurts".

**Journal entry from 9 July 2024**

*Been having trouble sleeping as anxiety stops me most of the time. With my son out late on the school holidays, I didn't get any sleep until around 2 am.*

Through all of it, my health was suffering and my identity as a mother was shifting. I used to believe that being a good mother meant anticipating problems and solving them. That if I paid attention, worked hard enough, and loved deeply enough, I could keep my children safe from anything.

This season taught me something far more confronting. I could not fix this, although I could sit beside it. I could advocate, monitor, organise, support, show up, and love without conditions. But I could not single-handedly remove the darkness.

### Journal entry from 2 August 2024

*Distressed call from my son this morning - he seemed to be having an anxiety attack about going to work. I left my work to rush home for the almost 2-hour drive, while talking to him on the phone most of the way.*

The journal shows the slow reshaping of me — from fixer to witness. From controller to steady presence. It is not a role I would have chosen, but it is one I have grown into. And threaded through it all, quieter but persistent, was hope.

Not dramatic hope. Not the kind that announces itself. Small hopes like hearing laughter, staying at school for the day or reaching out to me in the middle of the night to talk.

Hope built itself in the details. In noticing that even on heavy days, something still flickered. In realising that progress is rarely linear, but it exists.

### Journal entry from 31 August 2024

*Today I told my husband I had been feeling down. The conversation didn't go much further, and I didn't explain how heavy things have been feeling. Sometimes it's hard to find the words, even with the people closest to us.*

*In quiet moments, my mind drifts to difficult places. I catch myself wondering if somehow, I am responsible for the struggles my son is facing. Those thoughts can be heavy, even though I know deep down that mental health is far more complex than one person or one cause. For now, I remind myself of the people who need me here. My mum, especially. And so, I stay, holding on, hoping that tomorrow might feel a little lighter.*

On reflection, I can now see the weight of guilt I was carrying, which I still hadn't shared with those closest to me. At the time, it felt almost instinctive to blame myself, as if doing so might make the situation more understandable or controllable. Writing in my journal became a lifeline. On the page, I could acknowledge the fear, the heaviness, and the doubts without letting them take over my mind or my heart.

What began as a way to stop the blur became a mirror.

And in that mirror, I can see not just a mother in crisis — but a mother evolving. Learning to sit with what she cannot control. Learning that love is not about preventing every storm, but about staying when the storm comes.

***Dear Me,***

*I want to write to the mother who stayed.*

*The one who didn't leave the room, even when the fear was suffocating. The one who held her son's hand while the world felt like it had stopped. The one who counted breaths, scanned the hallway, and whispered reassurances she barely believed herself.*

*I see you.*

*I see the exhaustion etched into your bones, the trembling that hides behind a smile, the weight of responsibility that never lifts. I see the guilt you carried — guilt for what you couldn't prevent, guilt for every moment you weren't enough, guilt for laughing when your heart was breaking.*

*I see the isolation. That quiet ache that no one else could touch, the nights when the house was still but your mind never rested.*

*I see the anger, too. Not at your child — but at the unfairness of it all, at the world that doesn't understand, at a life that can shift so abruptly.*

*And yet -you stayed.*

*You stayed when it would have been easier to look away. You stayed when you wanted to run. You stayed when it would have been so tempting to convince yourself that someone else could carry it.*

*You stayed, and in staying, you bore witness. Not just to your child, but to yourself. To the courage you didn't know you had. To the love that is messy, unshakable, and terrifying. To the strength that isn't loud, but quiet and steady and unwavering.*

*Thank you for staying.*

*Because of you, your child knew someone was there. Because of you, the story didn't stop. Because of you, you discovered a depth of love and resilience you might never have known otherwise.*

*I hope you can look back now and allow yourself to feel what you carried — without shame, without judgment. Just acknowledgement. Just pride.*

*You stayed. That is enough.*

*Always,*
*Me*

## How to Begin to Journal and the Techniques of Journalling

Part of what makes journalling so meaningful for me wasn't just how it helped me process emotions—it was discovering that there is real science behind it. Neuroscience shows that putting our thoughts into words changes the way the brain works. When we write about our feelings and experiences, the thinking, rational areas of the brain communicate more effectively with the emotional centres, helping to calm the nervous system and allow clearer, more intentional thinking.

Dr Arif Khan, a neuroscientist and mental health expert, unpacks the science behind journalling. He points out that writing isn't just emotional release, but actual neurological repair. Through expressive writing, gratitude journalling and reflective reframing, you will discover how simple words can coordinate your brain's emotional and rational circuits, calm your nervous system and reshape your mind over time.

Over time, I noticed a subtle but important difference between typing my thoughts and writing them by hand. There is something in the slowing down, the connection to the page. As Dr Khan says, "Journalling is not just about what you write, but how you write it."

Handwriting has unique benefits compared with typing. When we write by hand, the brain engages motor, sensory, and cognitive processes simultaneously, which strengthens memory, deepens emotional processing, and slows us down enough to reflect more thoughtfully. Typing may be faster, but handwriting creates a more intimate, embodied connection to our thoughts, helping us truly process and integrate experiences rather than just recording them.

**Dear Handwriting,**

*I didn't always appreciate you. For a long time, I rushed past you—choosing speed over presence, typing over tracing my thoughts slowly onto a page. You felt too messy, too inconsistent, too imperfect to matter.*

*But somewhere along the way, I found my way back to you.*

*I began to notice how you asked me to slow down. How each word required intention, how each sentence unfolded at a pace my mind could follow rather than race ahead of. You held my thoughts differently—more gently, more honestly. There was no deleting, no editing in haste, just a quiet invitation to sit with what was real.*

*Through you, I found a deeper connection to myself. You carried my grief when I couldn't speak it, my confusion when I couldn't make sense of it, and my hope when it felt fragile. You didn't need to be neat or perfect—you just needed to be true.*

*There is something grounding about the way you move across the page.*

*The physical act of writing, of feeling pen against paper, reminds me that I am here, present, and capable of holding my own story. In a world that moves quickly, you offer me stillness.*

*Thank you for being a place where my thoughts can land. Thank you for reminding me that slowing down is not a weakness, but a way of understanding. Thank you for helping me come home to myself, one word at a time.*

*With gratitude,*
*Me*

Dr Khan explains that research shows that naming and writing down our feelings—a process called affect labelling—reduces activity in fear-driven areas of the brain while activating logical, planning regions. This not only calms emotional overwhelm but also frees up cognitive space, allowing us to make sense of experiences and respond thoughtfully instead of reactively.

Understanding this science deepened my respect for journalling as more than a reflective habit. Handwriting slows the brain down, increases emotional awareness, and helps thoughts integrate rather than loop. Handwriting became a practice that actively rewired my mind, helping me move from reactive survival toward a more thoughtful response, and giving me a way to engage with life's challenges with a steadier nervous system and a clearer perspective.

There are so many books, websites and beautifully curated journals that promise to teach you how to journal 'properly.' I don't think there is a wrong way to journal. You can find endless advice about prompts, structure, gratitude practices, and goal setting — all of it valuable in its own way. Heidi Swapp has some great classes, particularly the Introduction to Stop the Blur, which is a free class on her website.

But that isn't how this began for me. If I'm honest, I didn't sit down and decide, *Today I will practise a journalling technique.*

### 1. The Spill or Free Writing

It was much less organised than that. It was more like — *I can't carry this in my head anymore.* The way it came out depended on the day, and some days, I just needed to spill.

You know when your thoughts are racing, and you can't even separate one from the other? That's when I would just write without stopping. No structure. No paragraphs. Just whatever was circling in my mind. It didn't always make sense. Sometimes it was repetitive. Sometimes it contradicted itself.

But getting it out of my head and onto paper made it quieter.

This is also sometimes called stream-of-consciousness journalling. This involves setting aside a short amount of time, perhaps ten or fifteen minutes, and writing continuously without worrying about grammar, spelling, or structure. The goal is simply to let thoughts and emotions flow onto the page. Grief often lives in places that are difficult to articulate, and free writing allows those feelings to emerge naturally.

### 2. Unsent Letters

Other days, I found myself writing letters. Letters I never sent.

To my son — saying the things I couldn't say without making him feel responsible for my fear.
To people who minimised what was happening.
To myself, the exhausted version who was trying so hard to hold it together.

Letter writing is where you write letters to people, emotions, or experiences connected to your grief. These letters do not need to be sent or shared with anyone. You might write to the person you miss, to the part of yourself that is hurting, or even to grief itself. This can help externalise emotions and create space to express things that may feel impossible to say out loud.

There's something about starting with "Dear…" that changes the tone. It makes it personal. Direct. It turns swirling emotion into something you can actually speak. On paper, I allowed myself to speak the unspeakable. It gave my emotions a voice without consequence, without the fear of hurting someone or being misunderstood.

As you would have noticed, I have included some of these letters throughout this book.

**3. Reflective Journalling**

Reflective journalling involves writing about specific moments or memories and reflecting on their meaning. You might describe a difficult day, a memory that resurfaced unexpectedly, or a milestone that stirred old feelings. Reflecting on these experiences can help you notice patterns in your grief and recognise how your feelings shift over time.

This is often how I would capture my thoughts, and over time, it is a practice that builds your awareness. Over time, I have expanded my writing to explore the meaning of my words, how I am feeling, and the actions I may consider related to them.

**4. Listing**

Then there were the list days. Those were the days I couldn't handle emotion at all.

So, I would list facts.
Appointments.
Observations.

Naming emotions.
Questions.
Small wins.

Lists felt safe. Contained. They made the day feel manageable. Sometimes a list of tiny, almost insignificant things: 'he ate breakfast,' 'he went to work,' 'he stayed at school an extra hour' — was enough to remind me that not everything was falling apart.

### 5. Gratitude or Grounding Journalling

I have mentioned gratitude several times throughout this book, and I believe it is a daily practice that anyone can incorporate. At our dinner table, I would often ask my boys to share three things they were grateful for that day. It's true, as many have noted, that when you focus on gratitude, it becomes much harder to hold onto negative emotions at the same time — even for just a few moments, it creates a small but powerful shift in perspective.

This does not mean ignoring pain but rather allowing space to notice small moments of steadiness alongside the sorrow. Writing about a kind interaction, a peaceful moment, or something that brought even a small sense of comfort can help balance the emotional intensity of how you may be feeling.

### 6. Prompt-based Journalling

Prompt-based journalling can be useful when it feels difficult to begin. Prompts such as *What does my grief feel like today? What do I wish others understood about my experience?* Or *what has this journey taught me about myself?* can gently open the door to deeper reflection.

This is an approach I use in my daily journal – a place to ponder a thought or an opportunity to document deeper feelings about the prompt. There are many great books or websites that offer free journalling prompts. One book that encourages a creative practice for an inspired life is *The Book of Alchemy* by Suleika Jaouad.

This is a reflective and inspiring book about the art of journalling as a creative, life-nourishing practice. Rather than telling a single story, it combines Jaouad's own insights on writing with contributions from about 100 writers, artists, and thinkers, offering both essays and writing prompts to help readers engage more deeply with life's challenges and questions.

At its core, the book explores how journalling, something Jaouad has done since youth and through life's most difficult moments, can become a space for self-discovery, reflection, and resilience. She shares how keeping a journal helped her navigate illness, heartbreak, and uncertainty, and invites readers to see journalling as a tool for tapping into their own creativity and inner life. The book is structured around themes such as new beginnings, love, loss, and rebuilding, making it a companion for anyone dealing with transitions or emotional complexity.

Unlike a traditional self-help book with rigid steps, *The Book of Alchemy* blends meditative invitations with creative prompts that encourage readers to sit with discomfort, ask meaningful questions, and explore their truest selves. Contributors include well-known voices like Elizabeth Gilbert, George Saunders, and Jon Batiste, whose perspectives broaden the conversation about writing and creative life.

The book has been praised for its gentle encouragement and thoughtful design, appealing to lifelong journallers as well as those new to the practice. It focuses on embracing life's uncertainties and engaging with them creatively, rather than avoiding or suppressing them.

In essence, *The Book of Alchemy* offers both inspiration and practical reflection tools — not to fix life's problems, but to help readers sit with them, understand them better, and respond with creativity and curiosity.

Each way of writing met a different need, depending on how I was feeling that day.

The spilling was for emotion.
The letters were for relationship.
The lists were for control — or at least the illusion of it.

Some days the pages may fill with words, while other days there may only be a few sentences. Both are valid. The purpose is not to force healing but to create a compassionate space where emotions can be acknowledged and explored at your own pace. Over time, these pages can become a quiet record of resilience, showing how life experiences evolve and how the human spirit continues to move forward, even while carrying loss and challenging times.

I didn't realise it at the time, but I was meeting myself in layers and in the pages of my journal, allowing all of them to exist: the emotional one, the angry one, the controlled one, the hopeful one — without asking me to choose just one version of myself.

And sometimes, that's what writing really is - a place where all the versions of you get to sit down.

**Dear Journal,**

*Thank you. Thank you for being here, always, even when I wasn't sure I wanted to be. You have listened without judgment, held my messy thoughts, and carried the weight of my fears when I could not speak them aloud.*

*With you, I have been honest in ways I couldn't be with anyone else. I have spilled grief, frustration, anger, hope, and tiny sparks of joy across your pages. You have held my secrets and my truths, my questions with no answers, and my moments of clarity. In your silence, I have found reflection. In your blank pages, I have found space to breathe.*

*You have reminded me that my feelings are valid, that my experiences matter, and that even when life feels chaotic, there is a place where I can pause, look inward, and make sense of the storm. Thank you for being steady when I felt unsteady, for catching my tears in ink, and for allowing me to see myself more clearly, one word at a time.*

*I don't know where I would be without you, but I know I would be quieter, lonelier, and less brave. So thank you, truly, for being my companion, my mirror, and my confidant.*

*Me*

You know how sometimes you start something just to cope, and then one day you realise it's becoming something else? That's what happened with my journalling.

It wasn't just a place to spill anymore. I found myself slowing down. Choosing my words more carefully. Honestly, I was a bit tired of revisiting the same words repeatedly. Looking for meaning instead of just relief. I wasn't only trying to survive the story. I was trying to understand it and became increasingly curious about how to use writing for self-improvement and wellbeing.

That felt different. Focusing on gratitude, resilience and writing as a tool to overcome my anxiety. I started to think differently – how could I use my experience to give meaning and purpose to my life moving forward? I am a true believer that something good must come from a bad situation.

At first journalling was only for me – a private place to share my thoughts. Slowly, however, as time went on, I shifted from what I would call survival writing into reflection. I began to recognise compassion for myself and recognition that I was trying my best. After months of blame and shame, I began to soften the language I used toward myself, and reflecting on what I had written and how I had written it gave me a different perspective.

When I didn't have anyone to talk to, the pages gave me a place to stay present and that caring for others also meant I had to care for myself.

Using journalling as a tool allowing me to be the author of my life seemed inviting. Even in the darkest of times, writing allowed me to strengthen my thoughts and challenge the storyline in my head. Instead of feeling shame and guilt, how could I turn this around to create mindfulness and perspective I hadn't had before?

Let's delve a little deeper into my step into intentional writing for awareness and healing.

# CHAPTER EIGHT
# INTENTIONAL WRITING FOR WELLNESS

*"Questions are a quest for the mind"*

**Nicole Annette**

Nicole Annette is a writer, coach, teacher, and educator who focuses on intentional journalling as a tool for self-awareness, healing, and personal growth. She is the founder of *The Journal Coaching Co.*™, a platform designed to help people deepen their journalling practice with purpose and clarity rather than simply using a notebook as a passive space.

Her work centres on what she calls the *Journal Coaching Framework*™, which posits that thoughts influence emotions, emotions shape choices, and choices become the experiences of our lives. This framework helps people move from reactive thinking to intentional living through mindful writing and reflection.

Nicole hosts *The Journal Coaching Podcast*™, where she shares insights into how journalling can be used as an *intentional self-coaching tool* for clarity, emotional regulation, self-trust and leadership. The podcast has been active for several years and includes discussions on topics such as authenticity, emotional balance, and journalling with purpose.

She also teaches journalling practices to people who want to use writing as a reflective and transformative tool. Her teaching often emphasises self-awareness, storytelling, mindful writing habits and how internal reflection can bring about real change in people's lives.

Meeting Nicole and attending her online *See Yourself Clearly* two day writing workshop has been life-changing for me. Nicole emphasises that learning as an adult is all about making *meaning* of your experiences, and journalling helps you do that. I have always been a keen learner, so this seemed like a natural step to build further awareness of how to use my words differently to move me forward.

From building your own self-awareness and it then making a distinct difference in every season of your life, Nicole says, you cannot heal, grow or change if you cannot see the season you are in.

I recommend you explore Nicole's website and social media platforms (links at the end of the book), but when I participated in Nicole's *The Journal Coaching Field Study* course, which was a guided learning experience in awareness, belief and becoming, it hit home that the narrative of my life is within my control. I can influence, impact and change the stories I tell myself about my life.

I also read GG Renee Hill's *Story Work: Field Notes on Self-Discovery and Reclaiming Your Narrative,* which was like holding up a mirror to my own experiences. Hill writes about the stories we carry—those handed down to us, the stories we tell ourselves, and those that shape how we see the world. Her work reminded me that these narratives, no matter how heavy or painful, are not fixed. They can be observed, questioned, and even rewritten.

As I explored journalling more deeply, I found Hill's approach also resonated with me. Each page became a space to examine the stories I had been living—about myself, my parenting, my son, and the challenges we faced. Where I had once felt trapped by guilt, fear, or self-judgment, journalling offered a way to pause, reflect, and reframe. It wasn't about erasing the past, but about *choosing how I engage with it,* and discovering the threads of resilience, hope, and learning woven through it all.

Hill's prompts and reflections encouraged me to treat my experiences as material for growth rather than proof of failure. Her work helped me see that telling my story—and even rewriting it in small, intentional ways—is a powerful act of agency and self-care. In many ways, *Story Work* became both a guide and a companion on my journey to reclaim my voice, honour my experiences, and share them authentically with others.

Reframing my thoughts didn't happen all at once. For a long time, and even still today sometimes, my mind runs on autopilot, replaying fear, guilt, or self-criticism without pause. I would think *I should have done more,* or *this will never get better,* and I feel those thoughts as if they were facts. It took time to notice that they weren't truths—they were just stories my mind had learned to tell.

I started by paying attention. I must point out that I was still journalling daily with many of the techniques we have already mentioned in the book, but I began to catch myself when a negative thought arose and quietly ask myself, "*Is this the only way to see this?*" Or "*am I being fair to myself?*" Then, following Nicole's *Journal Coaching Framework*, I practised looking at the same situation differently. If I noticed self-blame, I asked, "*What have I actually done that shows care or effort?*" If fear crept in, I tried, "*What evidence do I have that things could turn out differently?*"

Writing became my ally. Journalling allowed me to slow my thoughts, lay them out on the page, and respond to them with compassion, as if I were speaking to a dear friend. Some days it was messy, but over time it has become a habit. I was learning to pause, to notice, and to gently reframe the narrative I was telling myself.

This process didn't erase the pain. It didn't mean everything suddenly felt okay. But it allowed me to see hope alongside grief, progress alongside setbacks, and strength alongside vulnerability. Reframing my thoughts became a way of telling a truer story—one that included not just the fear and the mistakes, but also the resilience, love, and courage that had quietly carried me through.

For me, my journal, as I have mentioned before, was a space to show up and keep me going. As I have moved through the events of the past few years, my journalling has evolved and continues to evolve. I write daily, considering what and how I write to process my emotions, feelings, and the world around me.

Listening to Nicole's podcast and completing her online courses makes the focus of 'purpose journalling' when writing through a life change or transformation, powerful. Nicole says, "Life is filled with unanswered questions and the courage to seek those answers gives meaning to life." The focus is on our stories as the narrative of our lives and on how we can seek to notice, explore, and understand them.

This really struck a chord with me, because after this period of ill mental health—for both my son and me—I found myself thinking many times, *So, this is now part of my story.* To be completely honest, I never wanted suicide, depression, or anxiety to be part of my story. Who would? And yet, at that turning point, I asked myself: *What am I going to do about this?* Recognising that this is no one's fault, we are human, after all, I began to see the possibility of learning, growing, and sharing from this experience.

Nicole's words echo in my mind… "At any moment, you can make a single decision which will change your present story". My future story is fully in my control. With every conscious or unconscious choice, I am planting a seed that will inevitably bloom in the future.

Nicole's *Journal Coaching Method Framework* is based on the premise that your story is trying to teach you something. Writing is more than expression; it is transformation, and true growth happens not from inspiration alone, but through reflection, learning, action and integration.

Nicole helped me see that when you use journalling to notice the loops in your thinking, the same fears, assumptions, and self-blame, you create a small opening.

Before that, the thoughts just felt true. Automatic. Unquestioned.

But when you write them down, you can see them. The repetition. The pattern. And once you can see the loop, you can pause it and interrupt it.

You can choose to place a different thought beside it, not a forced positive, not denial; just something truer. Something more balanced.

Instead of *"This is my fault,"* I can say, *"I'm doing the best I can with what I know."*

Instead of *"This will never change"*, maybe say *"Today was hard, but it isn't the whole story."*

That small shift doesn't magically fix everything. But it changes the tone of the story you are telling yourself. And when you change the story, even slightly, you begin to change the outcome or at least the way you walk through it.

Our thoughts often run in circles. The same worries. The same fears and the same stories are playing over and over. Those cycles keep going until something stops them; that something is awareness.

Writing helps you pause. Putting your thoughts on paper lets you see them more clearly instead of being swept along. You notice the pattern, the repetition, the loop.

And once you see it, you have a choice. You can question it. You can change it.

Writing gives you that space, and in that space, something new becomes possible.

Journalling for expression or to get down your thoughts is absolutely fine too. Now, I see this as the beginning– to release emotion is very helpful, but the next steps for me were to ask myself how my words were shaping my life. In the *Journal Coaching Podcast*, Episode 52, Nicole talks about inviting awareness as you enter the writing process. Being intentional and clear about what you want to get out of the writing session enables you to move closer to the outcome you desire. We can ask our journalling practice to help answer key questions.

*The Journal Coaching Method* that Nicole teaches include five core steps – Explore, Clarify, Plan, Activate and Reflect. Be sure to check out Nicole's online courses and resources for more details. The Reflect Stage has been critical to my wellbeing.

The Reflect stage of the *Journal Coaching Method* is about pausing and looking back — not just at what happened, but at how you felt, how you reacted, and what changed along the way.

You can access Nicole's teaching and reflections on her podcast series *The Journal Coaching Podcast,* but one of my biggest takeaways and something I try to remember in my journalling moving forward are these questions.

*"What am I noticing?"*

*"What does it mean"?*

*"What can I try?"*

*"What did I learn?"*

Nicole reminds us that reflection isn't a luxury or an extra. It's essential. It's part of taking care of yourself and supporting your own wellbeing.

The words we choose in our journalling reveal how we see life and what meaning we attach to our experiences. Nicole explains that this kind of deeper journalling can reveal emotional patterns, fear, and pain you haven't questioned yet.

***Dear Nicole,***

*I want to thank you.*

*Your words about reflection — that it's not a luxury but a necessity — have stayed with me. They came at a time when I didn't even realise, I had stopped noticing myself. When life was so full of doing, reacting, surviving, I forgot to pause, to look back, to see who I was becoming in the middle of it all.*

*What you taught me through the Journal Coaching Method, to slow down, to notice, to reflect — has been quietly transformative. It's helped me see patterns I couldn't see before, to give myself space to breathe, and to treat my own wellbeing with the same care I try to show my children.*

*Sometimes the simplest ideas are the hardest to remember: pause, notice, reflect. Yet your guidance made it possible to weave that into daily life, even in the middle of chaos.*

*I'm grateful for the clarity, for the tools, and for the permission to hold myself gently in the process.*

*With gratitude,*

*Me*

As I practised noticing and reframing my thoughts, writing quietly became more than a tool for processing grief or fear—it became a doorway to curiosity. What began as journalling to untangle emotions grew into an urge to explore the stories beneath those emotions, to look at life, relationships, and patterns in a new way.

I began experimenting with writing letters I would never send, reflecting on moments that unsettled me, and capturing the small, ordinary details of each day. Each page offered insight not just into what I felt but also into who I was, how I responded, and how I might grow.

Through this process, I realised that words could be more than documentation, they could be exploration, discovery and healing. Journalling had shown me that telling my story, fully and honestly, was not just about making sense of my own life, but about connecting with others, sharing experiences, and finding meaning in the messiness of being human.

As I explored writing more widely, I noticed something surprising: the pages of my journal were not just helping me understand myself; they were holding pieces of stories that might also matter to others. The small reflections, the letters, the exercises in reframing my thoughts, all pointed to a deeper desire to share. I realised that what had started as a private practice could become something public, a way to connect with people who might feel alone in their own struggles.

The idea of writing a memoir slowly took shape. It was not about creating a polished, perfect narrative; it was about honesty. About showing the messy, complicated journey of life with mental health, grief, and care, and the ways we find hope in the middle of it. I wanted to tell the story of survival, reflection, and learning; not just for myself, but for anyone who might recognise a piece of their own experience in these pages.

This practice opened a door I hadn't expected, curiosity about writing more widely.

Changing narratives, I realised, is a process. It begins with noticing the stories we tell ourselves, questioning whether they are true or helpful, and then gently reshaping them. Journalling gave me a safe space to practice this repeatedly, to explore different perspectives, and to give voice to parts of my experience that had previously gone unacknowledged.

Eventually, this curiosity and practice led me to write a memoir. I understood that my story, once something I wished I could hide, was worth sharing. Not because it was perfect, but because it was real. Because it reflected the messy, complicated, and ultimately human journey of care, grief, and resilience. Journalling, reframing, and consciously changing narratives had not only helped me process my own life; they had also given me a way to turn my reflections into something that could connect with, comfort, and inspire others.

When you give it a go, ask yourself why are you writing? Yes, getting your thoughts down is helpful, but you need to bring attention to the page. Purpose gives journalling meaning.

CHAPTER NINE

# LESSONS IN PARENTING AND SELF-CARE

As I moved through this experience, I began to realise that the lessons I was learning about parenting were deeply connected to what journalling was teaching me about myself.

You don't get to bloom without first facing the dirt.

## Grief

Grief changes your understanding of life. When you have experienced profound loss, you begin to see how fragile everything really is. The illusion that we can protect the people we love from every harm slowly gives way to a more complicated truth: love does not always mean control. Sometimes it means standing beside someone in their pain, even when you cannot fix it.

Losing our baby boy taught me that life can shift in an instant. It taught me that the future we imagine is never guaranteed, and that the moments we share with our children are more precious than we often realise in the rush of everyday life.

So, when this suicide attempt occurred, that earlier grief didn't make the situation easier. But it had already taught me something about endurance. I knew what it meant to survive something unimaginable. I knew that even when life fractures, there is still a path forward—though it may not look anything like the one you expected.

That experience also taught me something about how grief moves through families.

When our baby died, my husband and I were grieving the same child, but our grief didn't always look the same. I carried the physical memory of pregnancy and birth. My body had known this baby in a way that was deeply personal and difficult to put into words. My husband carried his grief differently - quieter perhaps, less visible, but still deeply felt.

Sometimes we leaned into each other. Other times, we stood beside one another in silence, each trying to find our way through the same storm.

Years later, through this event, I noticed those differences again. Parents often respond to a crisis in different ways. One may want to talk through every detail, while the other processes things internally. One may search urgently for solutions, while the other sits longer with the emotional weight of what has happened.

At times, this can feel confusing, even isolating. But eventually I came to understand that these differences are not a sign of distance or lack of care. They are simply different expressions of love.

I also learned that grief and fear can move through a marriage in different ways. While I often needed to speak about what I was feeling, my husband sometimes held his thoughts more privately. At first, those differences were hard to understand, but over time I realised that we were both carrying the same love for our child, simply expressing it in different ways. Staying connected meant giving each other space to cope in our own way, while remembering that love was still quietly holding us together.

What both experiences ultimately taught me is that resilience in a family is not about having all the answers. It is about staying connected in the face of uncertainty, allowing space for different ways of coping, and remembering that love often holds people together in quiet ways we do not always recognise in the moment.

**Hypervigilance**

After the crisis, I noticed something had changed in the way I moved through the world as a parent. I became more alert than I had ever been before. I listened carefully to the tone in conversations. I paid closer attention to mood changes, behaviour, even small shifts in routine. Silence sometimes felt louder than words.

At the time, I wondered if I was becoming overly anxious or protective. Later, I learned that what I was experiencing had a name: hypervigilance.

Hypervigilance is when the nervous system remains on high alert after a traumatic event. It is the body's way of trying to prevent harm from happening again. For parents who have lived through a mental health crisis with their child, this response can feel particularly strong. Our instinct to protect is already deeply wired within us, and experiences like this amplify that instinct.

In some ways, that heightened awareness helped me. It made me more attentive and more present. But it also came with a cost. Living in a constant state of alertness is exhausting. It can make it difficult to rest, relax, or trust that things are okay in the moment.

Understanding this helped me treat myself with more kindness. My body was not overreacting. It was trying to keep my child safe. Over time, I learned that healing also meant gently teaching my nervous system that it did not have to stay in survival mode forever.

One of the most surprising things I learned through this journey was how much the body remembers.

Even when I tried to stay calm on the outside, my body often told a different story. Tight shoulders, shallow breathing, fatigue, and a constant sense of tension became familiar companions.

It took time for me to realise that trauma is not only something we think about. It is something we feel physically as well.

When the nervous system experiences prolonged stress, the body holds that experience in different ways. Muscles tighten, sleep patterns change, and the mind can become trapped in cycles of worry and anticipation.

For parents navigating their child's mental health struggles, this physical response can become part of daily life without us even recognising it. Learning to notice these signals became important for me. When I felt my body tightening or my thoughts racing, it was often a sign that I needed to pause.

Journalling helped me do that. Writing slowed my thinking and allowed me to release some of what my body was carrying. It became a gentle way to tell my nervous system that it was safe to rest, even for a little while.

**Understanding ADHD in Hindsight**

Retrospectively, there are many things I wish I had understood sooner about ADHD. For a long time, I saw only the behaviours—the distraction, the unfinished tasks, the emotional outbursts. What I didn't see was the effort behind it all. I didn't realise how hard my son was trying just to keep up with a world that seemed to run at a pace his mind struggled to match.

I wish I had known that ADHD is not simply about attention. It affects emotions, motivation, organisation, and self-confidence. What sometimes looked like resistance or laziness was often overwhelm. What seemed like avoidance was sometimes fear of failing again.

I also wish I had understood the emotional weight ADHD can carry. Repeated corrections, missed expectations, and comparisons with others can slowly build a quiet sense of shame. A child can begin to believe that they are somehow not good enough, even when they are trying their very best.

If I could go back, I would spend less time worrying about getting everything right and more time focusing on connection. I would remind myself more often that progress is rarely linear, and that growth often happens in small, quiet ways that are easy to miss in the moment.

Most of all, I wish I had known that understanding ADHD sooner would have changed the lens through which I saw my son. Instead of asking, *"Why can't he do this?"* I might have asked, *"What is making this hard for him, and how can I help?"*

Alongside all of this came a quiet but significant realisation: success is not linear.  I think I am now a little easier, a little softer around the edges.  I try not to sweat the small stuff, letting things go more easily now.

For most of my life, I had held a very clear picture of what success was meant to look like, or so I thought. You do your best at school, you graduate, you go on to university, and you build a stable, long-term career. It was a path I had come to expect for myself and for my children.

But I began to understand that this pathway does not fit everyone, particularly for those navigating neurodiversity, such as ADHD. The traditional structure of school, with its expectations around focus, consistency, and routine, can be incredibly challenging. The same applies to the idea of a conventional full-time job, which often demands a rhythm and capacity that doesn't align with how some people naturally function.

That became our reality.

Through my son's experience, I began to understand that work doesn't have to follow a traditional path to be meaningful or successful. For someone with ADHD, the environments that are often held up as the 'ideal', such as structured classrooms, long hours, and rigid routines, can feel exhausting rather than enabling.

When he left school partway through Year 11, I worried about what that meant for his future. But what unfolded instead challenged everything

I thought I knew. He completed a short course, moved into an aged care traineeship, and began working across several part-time roles. What became clear was that this way of working suited him far better.

The flexibility allowed him to manage his energy and sleep patterns, and the variety kept him engaged. The human connection in his work: supporting others, interacting with people, seemed to give him a sense of purpose that a traditional classroom never quite could.

It made me realise that for someone with ADHD, work is not about fitting into a predefined structure, but about finding an environment that works with the way their brain functions. Roles that offer movement, variety, and connection can bring out strengths that might otherwise go unseen.

Watching him navigate this path shifted my perspective entirely. What I had once seen as a deviation from the norm, I now see as a more aligned and sustainable way forward. It reminded me that success is not about following a single path; it is about finding the one that allows you to function, contribute, and feel a sense of purpose in your own way.

**A Carer Identity**

Caring for someone through mental ill health is not something most people prepare for. It may happen gradually, often without a clear beginning. It can happen very quickly too, with one day not being like the next. One day, you are simply a parent, a sibling, a partner, or a friend. The next day, you realise you are also something more. You are coordinating appointments, making phone calls, researching services, and trying to understand systems that feel complicated and overwhelming. Somewhere along the way, you have stepped into the role of carer.

For me, this role became even more complex because the mental health challenges were not the only thing we were navigating. There were additional needs, layers that required support from different places. These include health services, education, community supports, and sometimes systems that did not seem to speak to one another. It often felt as though I was standing in the middle, trying to connect pieces of a puzzle that had been scattered across different rooms.

The emotional side of caring was one thing. Sitting beside someone you love while they struggle is its own kind of weight. But the practical side of caring can be just as demanding. The appointments, assessments, referrals, and waiting lists quickly become part of daily life. I found myself repeatedly explaining our situation to different professionals, hoping each conversation might lead to the support we needed.

What I began to understand during this time was how much carers do behind the scenes. We hold knowledge about the people we love that cannot always be captured in reports or forms. We see the small signs when things are improving and the quiet signals when something is wrong. We know the history, the personality, the strengths, and the vulnerabilities. Yet sometimes it can feel as though that knowledge is overlooked within systems that are already stretched.

There were also moments when I realised how easy it is for carers to forget themselves. When someone you love is struggling, your focus naturally shifts toward their wellbeing. Your own needs become secondary. You push through exhaustion, worry, and uncertainty because that is what love asks of you in those moments. But over time, I learned that carers need support too. Not because we are failing, but because caring is demanding, emotionally and practically.

Looking back, I can see that the role of carer was never something I chose; I stepped into it because it was needed. It required patience, persistence, and a willingness to navigate unfamiliar paths. More than anything, it required love; the quiet, steady kind of love that stays present even when the road ahead feels uncertain.

This has opened opportunities for me to provide a unique form of insight that professionals and even other family members may not immediately see. Carers understand the daily patterns, triggers, strengths, and vulnerabilities of the person they support. Their perspective can be invaluable when planning care or identifying what supports will work in everyday life. When carers are included as partners in care, rather than observers on the sidelines, the outcomes for everyone involved are often stronger and more sustainable.

Support for carers, therefore, needs to be both practical and emotional. Practical support may include guidance on navigating services, assistance with advocacy, and information about rights and available programs. Emotional support is equally important, offering carers the opportunity to speak openly about their experiences, share their concerns, and connect with others who understand the unique pressures of supporting someone with complex needs. There are many wonderful organisations that support carers, and I would encourage you to look them up within your local area.

Carers also benefit from opportunities to learn strategies that help maintain their own wellbeing. Caring for someone with multiple support needs can be demanding and unpredictable, and without time for rest and reflection, the role can quickly become exhausting. Recognising carers as individuals with their own needs, not simply extensions of the person they support, is an important step toward building a more compassionate and effective system of care.

Ultimately, supporting carers means recognising the vital role they play in the lives of people experiencing mental ill health and additional challenges. When carers are supported, informed, and included, they are better able to provide the steady, compassionate presence that so many people rely on during difficult periods of their lives.

In summary, here are some points about what it may mean to care for someone with ADHD.

**1. The Invisible Labour**
Caring for someone with ADHD often involves constant mental tracking—reminders, planning, anticipating, supporting emotional regulation. It's not always seen, but it's always there.

**2. Emotional Intensity**
ADHD isn't just about attention. It can involve big emotions, quick reactions, and sensitivity. Supporting this requires patience and calm, even when you feel overwhelmed yourself.

**3. Letting Go of Control**
Learning when to step in and when to step back can be one of the hardest parts. Growth often comes from allowing space, even when it feels uncomfortable.

**4. Advocacy and Misunderstanding**
You may find yourself explaining, defending, or advocating—helping others see beyond behaviour to understanding.

**5. Celebrating Strengths**
Creativity, humour, empathy, energy, and different ways of thinking are often part of ADHD. Noticing and nurturing these is just as important as managing challenges.

**6. Caring for Yourself**
Supporting someone else requires your own regulation, rest, and support. This is often learned the hard way.

Caring for someone with ADHD is not always visible from the outside. It lives in the small, everyday moments—the reminders, the quiet redirection, the effort to stay calm when emotions rise quickly and unexpectedly. It is a constant balancing act between supporting and stepping back, between guiding and allowing space for independence to grow.

I came to understand that ADHD is not just about focus or attention. It is about emotion, energy, and the way a person experiences the world.

**Curiosity**

The shift from frustration to curiosity has been one of the most important lessons of this journey. And it is a lesson I continue to learn every day.

I have learned that healing is not only about changing our thoughts. It is also about allowing the body time to feel safe again. And that takes patience.

Writing slowed my thinking down. It allowed me to step outside the constant swirl of fear, guilt, and responsibility and see my thoughts more clearly. When everything felt overwhelming, the page became a place where I could pause, breathe, and untangle what I was carrying.

Over time, I noticed something important: the same patience and curiosity I was learning to offer myself on the page was exactly what my son needed from me in real life.

Journalling taught me to listen without immediately trying to solve. It taught me to sit with difficult emotions rather than push them away. It taught me that understanding takes time.

Those were lessons I needed as a parent and only fully understood in hindsight. I can recall countless times sitting in an uncomfortable, almost frozen state, hearing words and cries I didn't know how to respond to. Emotions spilled out in ways I couldn't contain or make sense of, and for a long time, I stayed silent.

At first, I thought silence was the only option. I didn't have the right words, the right actions, or even the understanding to navigate what was happening. But as I began journalling, reflecting on these moments, I discovered that the silence itself held meaning. It forced me to slow down, to notice, and to really be present.

Writing became a way to process the discomfort; to explore the emotions I didn't know how to name in the moment. Through reflection, I started to see that parenting isn't about having all the answers. It's about showing up, holding space for your child's feelings, and trusting that presence itself can be enough.

Those moments of uncertainty became lessons in patience, empathy, and resilience. I learned to lean into the discomfort rather than run from it, to observe and reflect, and to carry those insights into the ways I engaged with my child and with life more broadly. Journalling didn't just help me process what I couldn't say, it helped me grow into the parent I wanted to be, one step at a time.

Before this, I often believed my role was to step in quickly, to fix problems and move us forward. But writing helped me see that some experiences cannot be rushed. Some feelings need space before they can be understood.

The page became my practice ground. It was where I could release the fears I didn't want to place on my family, explore the questions I was afraid to ask out loud, and reflect on the kind of parent I wanted to be in those difficult moments.

Instead of reacting out of panic or exhaustion, journalling helped me respond with greater awareness. It didn't make the journey easier, but it made me more present within it.

In many ways, journalling helped me parent more gently, not only with my children, but with myself as well. It helped set life events into perspective and enabled me to see just how I would like to live moving forward. In some ways, it allowed me to explore feelings I had kept bottled up for many years and make choices about how I would turn up in the world moving forward.

That may be one of the most important lessons this journey has given me: that reflection creates understanding, and understanding creates compassion.

When I look back on this time now, I can see how much it changed me, both as a parent and as a person.

There were moments when everything felt fractured. My thoughts, my confidence, my sense of certainty about how life was supposed to unfold. The experience shook the foundations of what I believed parenting looked like and what strength was meant to feel like.

But slowly, through reflection, writing, and learning to understand what my body was experiencing, something shifted.

I began to see that my nervous system had been doing exactly what it was designed to do: protect, respond, and stay alert in the face of something deeply frightening. What once felt like weakness or overwhelm was, in fact, my body's way of trying to keep my child safe.

**Resilience**

Before this journey, I thought resilience meant being strong, pushing through difficulties, and finding solutions quickly. Watching my son navigate ADHD and his mental health struggles taught me that resilience often looks very different.

Resilience can look like getting up and going to school on a day when everything feels overwhelming. It can look like trying again after a setback, even when the fear of failing is still fresh. Sometimes resilience is simply getting through the day.

There were moments when I saw how hard my son had to work to regulate emotions that arrived suddenly and intensely. I saw the effort it took for him to concentrate when his mind wanted to run in a hundred different directions. I watched how much courage it took for him to talk about feelings that were confusing or painful.

Through all of this, I began to realise that resilience is not about perfection. It is about persistence and continuing to show up even when things are difficult, uncertain, or uncomfortable.

My son also taught me that resilience grows best in environments where people feel safe, understood, and supported. When judgment is replaced with curiosity and criticism is softened with compassion, a young person can begin to trust themselves again.

I used to think I was the one guiding him through this experience. In many ways, that is true. But in equal measure, he has been guiding me by teaching me patience, empathy, and a deeper understanding of what strength really looks like.

What I have come to see is that resilience is not something we force into existence. It grows quietly in the spaces where love, understanding, and perseverance meet.

**What Journalling Taught Me About Parenting**

- Slowing down helps you see what is really happening.
- Not every thought needs an immediate solution.
- Listening—to yourself and your child—is the beginning of understanding.
- Emotions are signals, not problems to be eliminated.
- Reflection allows you to respond rather than react.
- Caring for your own mental wellbeing strengthens your ability to care for your child.

Journalling became the space where I could sit with that understanding. On the page, I could slow down long enough to notice what I was feeling, what I was carrying, and what I needed to keep moving forward.

It didn't remove the cracks that had appeared in our lives, but it helped me see them differently.

Like the Japanese art of kintsugi, where broken pottery is repaired with gold, the fractures themselves began to hold meaning. They became reminders of resilience, honesty, and the courage it takes to continue loving through uncertainty.

Parenting, I have learned, is not about keeping life perfectly intact.

It is about noticing the cracks when they appear, responding with care rather than blame, and allowing the healing to become part of the story.

The gold is not found in pretending nothing broke.

The gold is found in the willingness to repair, reflect, and remain present—repeatedly.

And sometimes, that quiet act of staying is the most powerful form of love we can offer.

CHAPTER TEN

# SO, WHO ARE YOU ANYWAY?

It's true, I will never be the same me. Everything in my life was impacted – perhaps not outwardly evidently to others, but for myself. The way I saw, and now see the world, my workplace and my performance were impacted, my confidence was rocked, and I was forced to rethink expectations and the future I had once hoped for. I felt like I had to rebuild who I was, all while supporting my son.

The discomfort of not living authentically became impossible to ignore, and it gently pushed me toward making the changes I needed.

One small but meaningful choice I made was to stop dyeing my hair. It may seem trivial to some, but for me, it became a quiet act of authenticity. Ever since my teenage years, I had coloured my hair to fit an image I thought I needed to maintain, to appear professional, polished, or acceptable in the eyes of others.

Letting go of that felt strangely liberating. I began to see the silver and brown strands not as signs of aging or imperfection, but as markers of experience, resilience, and the life I had lived. My hair became a reflection of who I truly was, rather than who I thought I should be.

Choosing authenticity in these ways reminded me that I didn't need to hide, mask, or conform to anyone else's expectations. It was a declaration that I could embrace myself fully, with all my quirks, flaws, and truths intact. And in that quiet, cumulative process, I found the courage to speak my truth, to live openly, and to align my outward life with my inner reality.

Authenticity doesn't have to be loud or dramatic. Sometimes it's small, personal acts such as a choice of hair colour, a preferred outfit, a commitment to self-care, which quietly transform the way you move through the world.

And when those choices add up, they become something profoundly freeing.

This experience had a profound impact on my career. I was in a senior management role that I genuinely loved, a position I had worked hard to build and one I took great pride in. For years, I had maintained a strong performance history and a deep sense of confidence in my ability to lead and support others.

But slowly, something began to shift.

I found that I could no longer sustain myself as I once had. The capacity I had relied on, including my focus, my motivation, and my ability to think clearly and make decisions, began to feel out of reach. I couldn't bring my full self to the workplace, and that was confronting. Supporting staff and managing the ever-growing demands of the role no longer felt natural, exciting or manageable as it once had.

As the pressure within the role continued, I reached a point where I felt completely depleted. It was an unfamiliar and deeply unsettling place to be. I could not give my team the energy and consistency of a leader that they deserved.

To be clear, my workplace was incredibly supportive in the aftermath of the initial crisis. They showed understanding and made accommodations where they could. But over time, it became evident that this level of adjustment could not be sustained indefinitely, either for them or for me.

What I hadn't fully grasped at the time was the extent to which everything I had experienced had impacted me. I had underestimated the emotional and cognitive toll it had taken. I struggled to put it into words, even to myself, let alone to others.

It is only now, with the benefit of distance and reflection, that I can see more clearly how it all unfolded or how it led to a point where I could no longer continue in the role as I once had. I was offered an opportunity to move into another role within the same organisation, and it was the best thing that could have happened. Not only was I able to utilise my creative talents in business development, but I also didn't have the pressure of supervising staff or overseeing financial responsibilities. I felt valued and could contribute in a way that was supported and meaningful.

One of the things I didn't understand at the beginning of this journey was how the experience was affecting my body. When my son tried to take his own life, the shock did not just affect my thoughts or emotions. It affected my nervous system. My body moved into what many people describe as survival mode.

Early on, I noticed it in small ways. My sleep changed. My mind raced, replaying conversations and moments repeatedly. My body felt tense, as if it was always waiting for something else to go wrong.

I later learned that this is a natural response when we experience something deeply frightening or traumatic. The nervous system is designed to protect us. When it senses danger, it releases stress hormones such as adrenaline and cortisol, preparing the body to respond quickly.

In short bursts, this response can be helpful. It sharpens our focus and gives us the energy to respond in an emergency. But when the threat is emotional, ongoing, or deeply personal—like watching your child struggle with their mental health—the nervous system can remain on high alert for much longer than it was designed to.

For parents, this can look like constant vigilance. A heightened awareness of every change in mood, every message, every silence. You may find yourself scanning for signs that something is wrong, even when things appear calm.

Your body is trying to keep your child safe.

The difficulty is that living in this state for extended periods can be exhausting. It can affect sleep, concentration, energy levels, and emotional resilience. You may feel anxious, overwhelmed, or physically drained without fully understanding why.  Looking back on my journal entries, I was often sick or feeling unwell – an upset tummy, aches and pain, tinnitus in my ears, headaches, etc.

Learning about this helped me have more compassion for myself. My reactions were not a sign that I was failing or not coping well enough. They were my nervous system responding to an experience that no parent ever expects to face.

One of the hardest parts of this journey was the weight I carried that very few people could see.

When a child is struggling with their mental health, parents often hold a silent responsibility that sits just beneath the surface of everyday life. Outwardly, the world continues as normal—work still needs to be done, meals still need to be made, conversations still happen —but internally, there is a constant layer of concern.

Questions sit quietly in the background of your mind.

*Is my child okay today?*
*Did I miss something yesterday?*
*Am I doing enough right now?*
*What happens next?*

These thoughts can become a steady hum beneath everything else. There is also a particular kind of guilt that many parents experience. The instinct to search backwards through time, examining moments and decisions, wondering if something could have been done differently.

Looking back, I realised how easily parents can place the entire burden of responsibility onto their own shoulders. We want so deeply to protect our children that when they are hurting, we instinctively look to ourselves for the reason.

But mental health is rarely that simple.

Children, like adults, move through a complex world of pressures, emotions, relationships, and internal struggles that cannot always be controlled or predicted. Understanding this did not remove my sense of responsibility as a parent, but it did help me see that love and care do not always prevent pain.

What matters most is how we respond once the cracks appear.

**Journal (partial) entry from 2 September 2025**

*Something that keeps coming up in my daily life and thoughts is who am I? A mother, a daughter, a wife, an employee...always going through the day thinking of what I need to do for others. I am not sure, but life events such as relationship changes have at times strengthened these roles. Events such as COVID and lockdowns really constricted my view of myself outside of the home. I didn't realise it at the time, but something has shifted more recently where I have been thinking about myself. Who am I beyond these roles? Who did I used to be? Is this what happens in midlife?*

*A change in my job role has given me back some self-confidence and belief in myself. That has flowed on to other life things...stepping back and saying no to being treated badly by some people has been hard but also empowering. What do I want my future to look like? Who do I want to be, and how do I want my kids to see me? It's like the world has opened up to me and I am seeing it again for the first time.*

*Writing daily, I am noticing more about my feelings, desires, and what I want, and it has helped me go out and seek it. Finding my passion, a job I enjoy and exploring who I am are exciting. Working on my physical health is next – feed the soul, feed the body. Attending to myself is just as vital as giving to others. Continuing to be kind to myself is key.*

I know it's often said, but I came to truly understand that life is too short.

Not in a cliché sense, but in a way that settled deeply within me and began to shape my choices.

One of the most significant shifts for me was recognising that if I wanted to continue growing, and if I wanted to hold on to a sense of positivity and possibility, I needed to be intentional about who I surrounded myself with. I needed people in my life who genuinely cared, lifted me, and made me feel safe being myself.

That realisation wasn't easy to act on. It meant making some clear and, at times, difficult decisions about stepping away from relationships that no longer brought me joy or alignment. There was discomfort in that, and moments of doubt, but also a quiet sense of clarity.

Somewhere along the way, I found a voice within myself—a steadier, more confident voice—that gave me the courage to make those changes. To set boundaries. To choose what felt right for me, even when it was uncomfortable.

And in doing so, I created space. Space for growth, for connection, and for a life that felt more authentic and aligned with who I was becoming.

Over time, I came to understand that carrying this invisible load did not mean I had to do so alone. Speaking about it, writing about it, and allowing others to support me slowly lightened the load.

It reminded me that behind many closed doors, there are families navigating similar journeys—quietly doing their best, learning as they go, and hoping for healing.

Sometimes the strongest thing a parent can do is simply keep showing up, even when the path forward is uncertain. And sometimes the bravest step is allowing yourself to put the weight down, even for a moment, and breathe.

In time, I began to realise that caring for my nervous system was an important part of caring for my family. For me, journalling became one of the ways I could gently regulate my thoughts and emotions. Writing slowed the constant mental loops and gave my mind somewhere to place the fears that had been circling endlessly.

Other small things helped too, such as breathing deeply, stepping outside for fresh air, talking to people I trusted, and allowing myself moments of rest when I could. None of these things solved the situation my son was facing. But they helped steady me enough to continue showing up.

I am still learning and working on this.

We touched upon Heidi Swapp's journey earlier in the book; she now has a podcast series called *The Shift*, co-hosted with Dr Vohn Watts. It focuses on making lifestyle and mindset changes, discussing women's health, and finding strength and purpose during midlife.

Heidi and her panel of speakers focus on building habits for sustainable lifestyles, unlocking the truth about brain health, hormones and healing the mind. The episode that resonated strongly with me was #004 – *Breaking Free from Fight or Flight: Healing the Nervous System.* This has become of particular interest to me, and something I am now beginning to explore more is the healing of the nervous system after a trauma such as this. I have been in a state of fight or flight for many years now, and it is terribly detrimental to all aspects of my life. I am a work in progress.

I began to realise that healing wasn't just in my mind, it was in my body too. Years of stress, grief, and worry had left my nervous system constantly on alert. My shoulders were tight, my heart raced, and even simple tasks felt exhausting.

Slowly, I continue to learn to respond with care. Deep breaths, gentle movement, quiet rituals, and journalling became ways to tell my body it was safe. As my nervous system softened, my thoughts became clearer.

Reframing worries, untangling emotions on the page, and noticing patterns all became easier when my body was no longer holding past tensions.

Healing, I discovered, is embodied. My mind, my body, and my heart all needed attention. Journalling helped me understand my story. Reframing helped me rewrite it. And tending to my nervous system helped me live it with presence, compassion, and a little more ease. Together, they became my quiet practice of wholeness, a way to move forward, step by step.

The raw panic and guilt that had dominated my days were slowly giving way to something steadier: awareness, patience, and a quiet confidence in my own capacity to cope and care. Journalling had been the tool, the mirror, and the teacher that guided me through this transformation.

I realised that resilience wasn't a heroic act but was woven through the small, consistent choices I made each day. Showing up when I was exhausted, listening when I was anxious, letting go when I wanted to control all added up, shaping the mother I was becoming. Through the pages of my journal, I could trace this evolution: from fear-driven reactions to mindful presence, from guilt to compassion, from isolation to connection.

The act of journalling also allowed me to reclaim parts of my identity that had been overshadowed by fear and responsibility. I remembered that I was a thinker, a highly competent professional, a woman capable of reflection and creativity. Writing daily, even in small fragments, reminded me that I could exist as both a mother and an individual, and that caring for my son didn't erase my own needs or aspirations.

I noticed a subtle shift in the way I approached challenges. Where I had once felt alone and powerless, I now carried a quiet trust in myself. Journalling had trained me to observe my emotions without being overwhelmed, to name them, and to respond with intentionality. This translated into parenting, yes, but it also translated into a broader resilience in life: the knowledge that I could face uncertainty, navigate fear, and still act with care and clarity.

I also recognised how much I had learned about vulnerability. Journalling taught me that acknowledging fear and grief didn't make me weak but made me human. By embracing my own emotions, I could model honesty and courage for my son. I could show him that life could be hard, terrifying even, and still be navigable. That connection, the shared experience of struggle and survival, became one of the strongest bonds in our relationship.

I have learned that speaking my truth, naming my anxiety, depression, and the difficult moments I have lived through, does more than give voice to my own experience. It opens a small door for others who may be struggling in silence.

At first, I worried about judgment or misunderstanding. I worried that sharing might make me feel exposed or vulnerable. But over time, I discovered something unexpected: the act of being honest, of acknowledging the full spectrum of my emotions, often resonates with others in ways I could never anticipate.

I am no longer afraid to talk about my experience. Each time I do, I hope it reminds someone that they are not alone, that their feelings are valid, that their struggles are seen, and that it is possible to navigate pain while still finding moments of hope. Speaking my truth has become both an act of courage and a quiet way of connecting, of offering comfort without needing to fix or solve anything.

Journalling didn't just help me survive the crisis; it reshaped who I am as a mother, a wife, and a person. It gave me tools to process fear, create space for connection, and nurture myself while caring for my sons. It reminded me that strength is quiet, resilience is built in small steps, and love is most powerful when it is patient, present, and persistent.

Through the pages, I discovered a mother who could hold both vulnerability and courage, fear and hope, pain and love. And in that discovery, I found not only a way to navigate the present—but a foundation for facing whatever the future might hold.

**Dear New Me,**

*I see you.*

*You are not the same person you were before. Life has asked more of you than you ever expected to give, and yet here you are—still standing, still loving, still learning.*

*There was a time when you believed parenting meant having the answers. You believed your role was to protect your children from every storm and guide them safely through life without too many scars. Now you understand something different. You know that parenting is not about preventing every crack, but about being present when those cracks appear.*

*You have learned to listen more deeply—to your children and to yourself. You have learned that silence sometimes holds more meaning than advice, and that sitting beside someone in their pain can be more powerful than trying to fix it.*

*You have also learned something you once struggled to accept that you matter too. Your wellbeing, your voice, your thoughts and emotions deserve space. Journalling gave you that space when you needed it most. It became a quiet companion, a place where your fears could land and where your strength slowly began to return.*

*Through writing, you discovered that reflection brings clarity, and clarity brings compassion. You became gentler with yourself. You allowed imperfection. You allowed truth.*

*You now understand that life, like the art of kintsugi, is not meant to remain unbroken. The cracks are part of the story. They are where growth begins, where resilience forms, and where the gold eventually appears.*

*The new you carries those cracks differently. Not as shame, but as wisdom.*

*Not as failure, but as evidence of love, endurance, and courage.*

*Keep listening.*
*Keep reflecting.*
*Keep showing up.*

*You don't have to be perfect to be a good parent, a good partner, or a good person. You only have to stay present, stay curious, and stay compassionate.*

*The journey continues, and you are stronger than you once believed.*

*With kindness and respect,*

*Yourself*

## Journalling as a Lifelong Anchor

Even now, years later, journalling remains a constant in my life, not because the crisis has ended, but because it taught me a way to navigate uncertainty, fear, and change with clarity and presence. What began as a tool for survival has become a lifelong practice, a quiet anchor that grounds me during life's unpredictability.

Dr Arif Khan, neuroscientist and mental health expert, has unpacked the science behind journalling and how writing isn't just emotional release, but actual neurological repair. Through expressive writing, gratitude journalling, and reflective reframing, you'll discover how simple words can synchronise your brain's emotional and rational circuits, calm your nervous system, and reshape your mind over time.

The pages remind me that reflection is a form of resilience. I continue to write not only about challenges, but also about growth, connection, and the small victories that can easily go unnoticed. Recording these moments allows me to see progress over time, reinforcing both my own capacity to cope and the strength of the bond I share with my sons.

Journalling has also become a way to process the ongoing, quieter fears that still arise. Life doesn't pause, and neither does anxiety, but putting words to it allows me to face it without being consumed. By observing my thoughts and emotions on the page, I can respond rather than react, approach challenges with intentionality, and remain present for my son without letting fear dominate the moment.

Beyond practical coping, journalling continues to deepen my understanding of myself as a mother and as an individual. It reminds me to hold space for both love and imperfection, for care and self-compassion, and for courage in the face of uncertainty. It reinforces that my presence matters more than perfection, and that resilience is built through consistent, intentional choices rather than dramatic gestures.

Most importantly, journalling has taught me that vulnerability and strength are not opposites. By naming my fears, doubts, and struggles, I have learned to model honesty and courage for my son. He sees me navigate emotions with intention and compassion, and through that, he learns to do the same. Writing has become a way to hold both our journeys without losing sight of either.

One of the clearest lessons was that presence matters more than perfection. In the months after my son's crisis, I learned that I could not control everything, nor should I try. What mattered was showing up, listening, observing, responding with care, and remaining steady even when fear threatened to overwhelm me. Journalling trained me to notice the subtle ways in which presence could support healing, both for my son and for myself.

Another lesson was the power of self-compassion. I had carried guilt and shame so heavily that it became a lens through which I saw every action, every decision. Writing allowed me to soften, forgive myself for my mistakes, and recognise that being human—imperfect, vulnerable, and sometimes overwhelmed—is not a failure. It was a necessary part of recovery, and a model for my children to see and learn from.

Journalling also taught me about the value of small, consistent choices. Recovery and growth were not dramatic leaps, but daily acts: pausing before reacting, acknowledging feelings, offering empathy, celebrating small victories, and maintaining routines. These choices accumulated over time, creating a foundation of trust, connection, and resilience that no single grand gesture could achieve.

Perhaps the most profound lesson was about connection—how it is nurtured, repaired, and maintained. Through journalling, I realised that openness, honesty, and presence were more powerful than any attempt to shield my children from life's difficulties. By showing them that fear and grief could be named, reflected upon, and managed, I gave them a model for navigating their own emotions, and for building trust and closeness even in the face of hardship.

Finally, I learned that healing is ongoing. Journalling is not a tool with a final endpoint; it is a lifelong practice. It reminds me that reflection, awareness, and self-care are not luxuries—they are necessities. The practice of putting words on the page strengthens my capacity to parent, to love, and to survive, long after the initial crisis has passed.

In this way, journalling is no longer just a practice of survival. It is a practice of living fully, loving deeply, and parenting with presence. It is a reminder that life, even after trauma, can be navigated with awareness, patience, and grace. And as long as I keep writing, I know I can face whatever comes next, anchored in both my own resilience and the enduring connection I share with my son.

Today, journalling is not just about processing trauma; it is about connection. Connection to my own experiences, to my children, and to the story of who I am becoming. It is a place where I can see the gold in the cracks, the Kintsugi of my life, and carry it forward as a tool, a companion, and a source of wisdom.

No matter what the future holds, the page remains. A constant. A reminder that even when life feels fractured, I have a space to pause, reflect, and anchor myself.

**The Power of Connection, Community and Belonging - Kintsugi Heroes**

There is a quiet strength that comes from finding people who really see you and hold space for your story without judgment. Discovering Kintsugi Heroes was more than joining a group; it was finding a community that understood, supported, and believed in me in a way that gave me courage I didn't know I still had. In their presence, sharing my story didn't feel like a risk anymore; it felt like an act of healing, a bridge between isolation and belonging, and a reminder that connection can be as transformative as any therapy or strategy.

Kintsugi Heroes is a movement and community inspired by the Japanese art of *kintsugi*. I have mentioned this previously throughout the book and really tried to write with this theme in mind. Kintsugi is the practice of repairing broken pottery with gold or precious lacquer so that the cracks become part of the object's history and beauty rather than something to hide.

In the context of mental health and resilience, Kintsugi Heroes uses that metaphor to show that people who have experienced trauma, struggle, or breakdown aren't 'damaged' in a way that needs hiding. Instead, their experiences, the cracks and repairs, are what give them strength, depth, and worth.

The core idea is that we are not damaged goods because we've been through hard things deeply resonated with me. It resonated with all the guilt, shame and secrecy I had been holding throughout this period. Kintsugi believes we are more luminous because of what we have survived. The cracks in our story can become the gold.

There they were: people who had lived through their own storms, who understood what it meant to walk through fear and come out the other side, sometimes bent but unbroken. I have listened to many podcasts as someone shared their story, and something shifted inside me. For the first time in a long time, I didn't feel alone. My story, the one I had been holding like a secret too heavy to share, suddenly felt safe.

I was also instantly drawn to the idea of kintsugi, the Japanese art of repairing broken pottery with gold so that the cracks aren't hidden but celebrated. There's something quietly radical in it: the cracks aren't flaws to erase; they are part of the history, part of what makes the piece whole and unique. Having had the opportunity to participate in a kintsugi workshop recently, taught by a true Japanese master, it really is a lesson in patience and perspective.

Repairing broken ceramics with lacquer and gold wasn't just about restoration, it reframed damage as part of an object's history rather than to conceal or discard all together. The process was slow, deliberate and unexpectedly meditative.

For me, journalling became a bit like kintsugi. Every raw thought I poured onto the page, every fear I named, every small victory I recorded, was the gold filling the cracks. They didn't make the pain disappear or undo the moments of fear, guilt, or helplessness. But they made those moments meaningful and made them mine.

Through writing, I started to see that the broken pieces in our lives, the moments that feel like they'll define us forever, don't have to remain hidden. They can be transformed into something strong, even beautiful. And just like kintsugi, it's not a quick fix; it's a careful, ongoing process.

In that sense, I began to understand what it means to be a Kintsugi Hero: to survive, to reflect, to repair, and to allow the gold to show. Not perfect, not untouched, but luminous in the truth of what has been lived and what continues to be built. I want to write to help others share their stories so those who need to hear them can find them.

Connection, I learned, isn't only about being in the same room. It's about being seen and understood, even through the smallest openings, such as a page, a podcast, a story that says, "You are not alone." And that understanding became the quiet strength that allowed me to begin sharing my own story.

Founder and CEO Ian Westmoreland has been instrumental in encouraging me to share my story, and through my involvement with Kintsugi Heroes, I recognise that, just because I may feel broken at times, it doesn't mean we cannot overcome adversity, rebuild, and reconnect to become something beautiful again. To become more powerful and meaningful to ourselves and others.

***Dear Ian,***

*I want to thank you sincerely for all that you do through Kintsugi Heroes. Your vision, leadership, and belief in the strength of people with lived experience of mental health challenges make a profound difference.*

*For me personally, your faith in my ability to share my story has meant more than words can express. Giving voice to my journey, the fears, the struggles, and the small moments of hope, was daunting. Yet knowing that you and Kintsugi Heroes value these stories and believe in their power to inspire and support others has given me courage I didn't know I had.*

*Your work reminds me that healing and resilience can coexist with pain, and that the cracks in our lives are not weaknesses but sources of strength and growth. Thank you for creating a space where stories like mine can be told with honesty, compassion, and purpose.*

*With gratitude,*

*Me*

The power of storytelling is rooted in my goals for this book, and I never imagined this story would be the start of my life as a writer. It is a transformative experience to be offered the opportunity to be seen, heard and appreciated. Kintsugi Heroes points out that this powerful exchange, when our stories inspire, uplift and empower audiences, is why storytelling remains central to their mission of improving mental health.

Why Kintsugi Heroes is so effective is that storytelling facilitates community engagement and resilience and supports individuals' wellbeing. They adopt storytelling as a central methodology in their programs, thereby effectively improving the mental health of Australians. It is my hope that through the partnership of Kintsugi Heroes, this book can do all it sets out to do.

By sharing my truth, vulnerability, and life experiences, I hope this book brings others true connection and hope. I will forever be grateful to Ian and Kintsugi Heroes for their support.

**Journalling, Healing, and the Gold in the Cracks**

Parenting through a mental health crisis changes you in ways you can't fully anticipate. There are moments when everything feels fractured and your confidence, your sense of safety, even your understanding of who you are as a parent. But slowly, through reflection, journalling, and learning to understand what my body was experiencing, something shifted.

I began to see that my nervous system had been doing exactly what it was designed to do: to protect, respond, and stay alert in the face of something deeply frightening. What once felt like weakness or overwhelm was, in fact, my body's way of trying to keep me safe.

Journalling became the space where I could sit with that understanding. On the page, I could slow down long enough to notice what I was feeling, what I was carrying, and what I needed to keep moving forward. It didn't remove the cracks that had appeared in our lives, but it helped me see them differently.

Journalling began as a tool for survival, a way to release the fears, the questions, and the exhaustion that came with parenting in crisis. Over time, it became a lifelong anchor—a steady point in the swirling uncertainty of life. Writing allowed me to notice patterns, reflect on my responses, and track the small victories that might otherwise have gone unseen. It became the bridge between my emotions and my actions, helping me parent with presence, respond with patience, and care for myself without shame.

Journalling doesn't have to be perfect. It doesn't need rules, neatness, or full sentences. A list, a letter, a single word, even fragments, are enough. Each time you put a thought on the page, you practice awareness and self-compassion. These small moments accumulate, creating a space where you can hold your fears, your doubts, and your fragile hope.

The cracks, the fractures, the moments that break your heart, they are not signs of failure. They are part of your story, pieces of the life you are living and learning from. And as kintsugi reminds us, it is in those very cracks that the gold can be placed: awareness, reflection, compassion, and courage, transforming what was broken into something stronger, wiser, and beautifully whole.

Parenting, like journalling, is not about perfection. It is about showing up, noticing, tending, and allowing the repair to be visible. It is about carrying love through uncertainty, learning from the cracks, and letting yourself be held by the gold that slowly forms in the spaces you thought were broken.

And sometimes, simply showing up is the most powerful form of love you can offer yourself and those you care for.

EPILOGUE

# REFLECTIONS ON THE JOURNEY

*"We've all had times when we've felt our spark fade. When happiness seems out of reach, by miles or by millimetres, the natural response is to adapt and keep on living. We lug around invisible weights, go through the motions of our day, smile, wave, and wonder if this is as good as it gets. The longer we live in this state of slow erosion, the more it feels like the only state there is. Sometimes we need a miracle to snap us out of it; other times it takes a tragedy. And sometimes, the sudden clarity can shock you into writing an entire book."*

**Campbell Walker** - *from his book Doom and Bloom*

Writing this memoir has been, in many ways, an extension of the journalling practice that carried me through the most difficult period of my life. It has reminded me that pain and fear are part of being human, but they do not define us. What defines us is how we respond, how we show up, and how we choose to hold both ourselves and those we love through life's challenges.

Journalling gave me a space to process emotions without judgment, to reflect without pressure, and to track growth even when it felt invisible. It taught me that resilience is not about being unshakable. It is about persistence, patience, and the willingness to keep moving forward, day by day, moment by moment.

Through this journey, I have learned that parenting is not about perfection or control. It is about presence, empathy, and creating an environment of trust and connection. It is about allowing children to be human and allowing ourselves to be human alongside them. It is in the small, consistent choices: listening, pausing, offering support, that real strength and healing are built.

I am still concerned about the future – not just for my son but for those of us who endure and choose to speak about mental health. A 2026 survey by the Australian Human Resources Institute found that around one-third of employers admitted to excluding candidates with mental illness during hiring processes. The same data shows that about 32% of employers have avoided hiring someone with a history of mental illness. Overall, 7 in 10 employers said they exclude candidates based on certain personal attributes, including mental illness, disability, or age.

Research shows that mental health in the workplace is both vital and fragile. Stigma remains a significant barrier, with many employees fearing disclosure and experiencing discrimination, which can worsen stress and isolation.

Reading the research helped me see that these challenges are not personal failings; they are systemic. And just as importantly, it reminded me that creating space for honesty, compassion, and support, both for myself and for others, is essential. Mental health, whether at work or not, is not an individual burden to carry alone; it is a shared responsibility that requires awareness, care, and courage.

I have certainly learned on a personal level, however, that love is powerful, but it is most effective when paired with self-compassion. Caring for others cannot come at the cost of losing yourself. Journalling taught me to hold space for both my son and me, to acknowledge my own vulnerability while offering steady care, and to embrace life's uncertainty with courage.

Here are my key takeaways in learning about myself and how to move forward:

1. Your nervous system is responding, not failing. Stress, fear, and trauma trigger natural survival responses—fight, flight, freeze, or fawn. Understanding this can help you respond with compassion for yourself.

2. Hypervigilance is normal after a crisis. Constant alertness is your body's way of protecting what matters most. Over time, awareness and self-care help regulate it.
3. The cracks are part of the story. Like kintsugi, broken moments are not failures. They are opportunities to notice, repair, and grow stronger.
4. Journalling is a powerful anchor. Writing slows mental loops, gives clarity, and allows reflection. It doesn't fix everything, but it creates space to process fear, hope, and love.
5. Parenting is about presence, not perfection. Showing up consistently, noticing the cracks, and responding with care matters more than having all the answers.
6. Self-care is essential, not optional. Caring for yourself, physically, emotionally, and mentally, allows you to show up fully for your children and for life.
7. Small steps create change. Reflection, writing, and gentle awareness gradually build resilience and a stronger sense of self.

Reflecting on the previous years, I can see that the most difficult moments of my life did not break me in the ways I once feared they would.

Losing our baby boy left a crack in my heart that will always be there. It is a quiet space I carry with me, a reminder of the son who should have grown beside his brothers, and of the fragility of life itself.

Years later, when my oldest son faced his own battle within his mind, another crack appeared. This one was different. It was not the silence of loss, but the terrifying possibility of it. The realisation that someone you love deeply can be standing right beside you and still feel unbearably alone.

For a long time, I thought these cracks meant something had gone irreparably wrong. That perhaps I had failed as a mother somewhere along the way.

But over time, through reflection and through the quiet act of writing, I began to see them differently.

Journalling gave me a place to pour out the fear, the guilt, the confusion and the grief that I could not always say aloud. It allowed me to slow down my thoughts, to notice patterns, and to sit with emotions that otherwise felt overwhelming. Word by word, page by page, the act of writing helped me hold the broken pieces of these experiences together.

In many ways, it reminded me of kintsugi — repairing broken pottery with gold.

The cracks are not hidden. They are honoured.

They tell the story of what has been broken and what has been repaired. They become part of the object's beauty rather than something to disguise.

My life as a mother now carries those golden seams. My lost baby's memory. My son's survival. The lessons learned through grief, fear, and love.

None of these experiences are ones I would have chosen. But they have shaped the way I see the world, the way I hold my children, and the way I understand the quiet strength that can grow from even the most painful moments.

The cracks are still there. But so is the gold. I have learnt that I am enough. I am enough to make my children secure.

If there is one overarching lesson, however, that I could leave with readers, it is this: even in the face of unimaginable fear, isolation, or crisis, there is a path forward. Reflection, presence, and deliberate care, whether through journalling or mindful practice, can guide us through the darkness, help us rebuild trust and connection, and reveal the resilience that lives quietly within us all.

This memoir is a testament not only to survival, but to growth, love, and the enduring power of presence. It is proof that even in the most difficult chapters of life, we can find a way to move forward—stronger, more compassionate, and more deeply connected to those we love.

So, what's next?

I have continued to deepen my knowledge through further study and research, building on my coaching qualifications with a particular focus on journal coaching. My passion is creating safe, supportive spaces where women, carers, and anyone interested in writing for wellbeing can explore their thoughts, process emotions, and reflect on their experiences.

If you feel drawn to this practice, I would love to invite you to join an online guided journalling circle or explore one-on-one journal coaching. Together, we can use journalling as a tool for clarity, growth, and self-discovery—helping you uncover your voice, reconnect with yourself, and navigate life's challenges with intention.

If this feels like something you would like to explore, I would love to hear from you by contacting me via my website at:

www.intentionalwritingforwellness.com

## RESOURCES

I've included these resources not as a comprehensive guide, but as a collection of the people, books, and programs that have genuinely supported me on this journey. I hope they can offer you comfort, guidance, or inspiration, too.

**Books & Journals** – memoirs, self-help, guided journals

*Dear Psychosis* by Sarah Martin

*The Great Book of Journalling by* Eric Maisel & Lynda Monk

*The Book of Alchemy* by Suleika Jaouad

*Story Work: Field Notes on Self-Discovery and Reclaiming Your Narrative* by GG Renee Hill

*Doom and Bloom – The case for creativity in a world hooked on panic* by Campbell Walker AKA Struthless

**Support Services** – helplines, mental health organisations, carer support

Headspace Mental health online support - 1800 650 890

Wellways Mental Health and Wellbeing Connect - Phone 1300 000 717

Everymind: Free online support for family and friends of someone who has attempted suicide

https://everymind.org.au/news/free-online-support-for-family-and-friends-of-someone-who-has-attempted-suicide

Lifeline Australia - 13 11 14

https://www.lifeline.org.au

https://www.suicideline.org.au

https://www.zerosuicide.com.au

Beyond Blue – 1300 22 4636

Suicide Call Back Service – 1300 659 467

https://www.carergateway.gov.au

https://www.carersaustralia.com.au

Carer Gateway - 1800 422 737

Carers Australia - 1800 242 636

**Online Communities** – forums, websites

www.kintsugiheroes.com.au

www.heidiswapp.com

www.youtube.com/@theshiftcollectivepod

www.youtube.com/@OGTherapy

https://thejournalcoachingcompany.mykajabi.com

https://www.instagram.com/thejournalcoachingco

https://www.drarifkhan.com

https://youtu.be/76HuH7Pm69k?si=xH9KnmsqB9Otkq-i

**Courses & Programs** – coaching, workshops, online learning

Introduction to Journalling Course Online | Learning Cloud Australia

Certified Course to Become a Journal Therapy Coach – Certified Excellence

The Journal Coaching Company™

## ACKNOWLEDGEMENTS

This book was not written in isolation, even though much of what it holds felt deeply personal at the time.

To my family — thank you for walking this path with me, even when none of us knew where it would lead. To my boys, you are at the centre of everything. You have taught me more about love, courage, and resilience than I could ever have imagined. It is a privilege to be your mother, in all the complexity that brings.

To my husband, thank you for your steady presence and quiet strength. In moments when everything felt uncertain, you remained grounded, offering support in ways that often went unseen but were always felt.

To the close friends who stood beside me, often without needing words, thank you for your presence, your patience, and for holding space when I could not.

To the professionals and support people who guided us through uncertain moments, your care and compassion made a difference that is not easily put into words.

To the community that surrounds Kintsugi Heroes, thank you for creating a space where lived experience is not only acknowledged but valued. There is something powerful in being part of a community that does not ask for perfection but instead embraces the cracks and the stories they hold. Your work reminds me that healing does not happen in isolation, but in connection — in being seen, heard, and understood.

And to those who may see parts of their own story reflected in these pages — this is not mine alone.

# ABOUT THE AUTHOR

Sarah Rosse holds a Bachelor of Social Science and several postgraduate qualifications, including a Certificate IV in Workplace and Business Coaching. With over 30 years of experience in the disability and care sector, she has dedicated her career to supporting people and families navigating complex challenges, combining professional expertise with lived experience as a parent and carer.

A passionate advocate for mental health and wellbeing, Sarah is also a Business Development volunteer with Kintsugi Heroes, helping to support and grow programs that empower Seniors, carers and people with lived experience. She is now exploring opportunities to expand her work into Storytelling Workshops, journal coaching and facilitated writing circles, combining her love of writing with her commitment to reflection, growth, and wellbeing.

When she's not writing, Sarah enjoys crafting, journalling, and spending meaningful time with her family. Her memoir is both a reflection of her journey and an invitation for others to explore their own stories with honesty, courage, and compassion.

www.ingramcontent.com/pod-product-compliance
Lightning Source LLC
LaVergne TN
LVHW050933210926
848482LV00013B/604
* 9 7 8 1 7 6 3 5 9 0 6 4 9 *